WITHDRAWN

ETHNIC IDENTIFICATION AMONG AMERICAN JEWS

Socialization and Social Structure

Arnold Dashefsky
University of Connecticut

Howard M. Shapiro
Dover Mental Health Associates
of New Hampshire

UNIVERSITY
PRESS OF
AMERICA

Lanham • New York • London

Reprinted in 1993 by
University Press of America®, Inc.
4720 Boston Way
Lanham, Maryland 20706

3 Henrietta Street
London WC2E 8LU England

Copyright © 1974 by Arnold Dashefsky and Howard M. Shapiro.

Originally published and copyrighted by D.C. Heath and Company.

Library of Congress Cataloging-in-Publication Data

Dashefsky, Arnold.
Ethnic identification among American Jews : socialization and social
structure / Arnold Dashefsky, Howard M. Shapiro.
p.   cm.
Originally published: Lexington, Mass. : Lexington Books, 1974.
Includes bibliographical references and index.
1. Jews—Minnesota—Saint Paul.   2. Social surveys—Minnesota—
Saint Paul.   3. Socialization.   4. Saint Paul (Minn.)—Social
conditions.   I. Shapiro, Howard M.   II. Title.
[F614.S4D37   1992]
305.892'40776581—dc20   92–15759 CIP

ISBN 0–8191–8333–4 (pbk. : alk. paper)

 The paper used in this publication meets the minimum requirements of
American National Standard for Information Sciences—Permanence
of Paper for Printed Library Materials, ANSI Z39.48–1984.

To Sandy and Shelley
and Michael and Alisa
and Lynne and Beth

The process by which Jews transmit their values and their commitment to group cohesion from generation to generation is poorly understood. However, the fact of this transmission cannot be denied.

Mortimer Ostow

Contents

List of Figures

List of Tables

Preface

In the 1970s it is not unlikely that the text of the rabbi's Rosh Hashanah sermon, the agenda of the Jewish Federation's leadership conference, and the policy statements of the prime minister of Israel may all have one common theme: Jewish identity. The question *What is a Jew?* attained importance about two hundred years ago when the social and physical walls of the European ghettoes crumbled under the impact of the French Revolution. The question *Who is a Jew?* achieved prominence two or three decades ago when the pain and suffering of the holocaust became the birth pangs of the Jewish State of Israel. These questions still are debated in the major Jewish communities throughout the world, so much so that one sociologist has remarked that the discussion of the issue of Jewish identity in itself may constitute a means of Jewish identification. Today, these questions have assumed a new significance for both Jews and Gentiles as a consequence of the international tensions surrounding Soviet Jewish emigration, the Yom Kippur War, and the relations between Israel and the other Middle East countries.

The voluminous and detailed literature about the Jewish people past and present is awe-inspiring. Historians, novelists, and essayists provide us with rich, perceptive accounts of Jewish identity, Jewish culture, and virtually all other aspects of Jewish life. Why then do we present an empirical study of only certain social psychological issues related to Jewish identity investigated among a few hundred respondents in one place and at one time? A complete answer would require an exposition and defense of the rationale of social psychology, and of survey research within this field. We believe that there are patterned commonalities and differences among groups and individuals which are rendered more understandable by systematic conceptualization and observation. This applies to ethnic identification among contemporary American Jews as well as to the myriad other issues and peoples that have been studied by social psychologists.

A word also about survey research on our topic. We believe that there are many ways to increase our understanding of Jewish identification —from autobiographical accounts of individual Jews to national surveys such as the National Jewish Population Study now being analyzed. In this study we have chosen what we believe is a useful middle ground by collecting the same type of information in some depth from about three hundred people in one community. This allows us to present a picture of the communal "life-space" in which most of our respondents have grown and currently live as well as letting us ascertain through questionnaire data something of the social patterns and individual characteristics relevant to their Jewish identification. While all communities are somewhat atypical, we agree with Goldstein and Goldsheider that such studies are necessary and useful (1968: 233-34).

Our primary goals are to contribute to an understanding of some basic social processes in general and the nature of Jewish life in particular by using the conceptual, methodological, and statistical tools of contemporary social science. By so doing, we hope to augment the valued contributions of more historical and psychological works. At the same time we hope our efforts will stimulate the further development of social science research in the social psychology of Jewish life in particular and ethnicity in general, as well as its application to the problems confronting Jews and other ethnic groups.

Preface to the University Press of America Edition

Grandpa Rosenthal was very proud of his granddaughter who was in her first year at Princeton. He was also intrigued with the courses the young woman was studying. "Tell me something," asked Rosenthal, "what is this sociology business all about?"

"Well, it is a comparatively new subject," the granddaughter began. "They didn't know much about it when you went to school."

"Nu, so enlighten me," said the grandfather.

"Sociology," explained the young woman in her best textbook manner, "is the science which deals with social phenomena; the systematic study of human behavior as a function of social structure and group life, and so on."

"And what does that mean in plain English, if I may be so bold?" asked the grandfather.

"Simply put, it means the study of how people act and what they do...."

"Oh!" Grandpa Rosenthal exclaimed, "so that is sociology! This is new by you? When I was a boy, we called it ordinary *yiddishe saikhel!*" (Jewish common sense.)

For Grandpa Rosenthal, sociology seemed to be nothing more than ordinary common sense. In the latter part of the twentieth century, we have come to learn that sociology provides the evidence to either support or refute ordinary common-sensical assumptions. Furthermore, social science in general can provide the data to answer questions about the nature of human behavior and attitudes. Indeed, such was the intention of our book: to empirically assess the sources and consequences of Jewish identification.

We approached this issue at a time, nearly two decades ago, when there was a heightened interest in all forms of ethnic identity in American society. The popular periodical literature about the Jews spoke a good deal about their identity and whether the Jewish people would endure. In fact, *Look* magazine wrote an article in the 1960s entitled "The Vanishing American Jews." Fortunately for the Jews, *Look* magazine vanished before they did! Despite such popular interest at the time of the first publication of this volume, research that assessed the nature of Jewish identity and identification was quite uncommon. Our work sought to contribute to eliminating the vast gaps in empirical knowledge about Jewish identity and identification.

Despite the passage of time, the issue of Jewish identity remains as relevant today as it was two decades ago. Perhaps this is all the more true given the rise in rates of assimilation and intermarriage. Indeed, there are many ways, from autobiographical accounts to national surveys, to understand Jewish identity. At the time of the original publication of our book, analysis was proceeding on the first National Jewish Population Survey. Today, as the second edition appears, a second National Jewish Population Survey of 1990 is being analyzed. The kind of analysis contained in our volume, however, is more systematic than relying on autobiographical accounts and more detailed since it focuses on a single community in its probing of Jewish identity than is possible with a large national survey.[1]

In looking back, we note a number of important issues that we helped to illuminate in our book that are still relevant today. First, we stressed the positive basis for shaping Jewish identification rather than the negative basis of anti-Semitism and outgroup prejudice and discrimination that were so often emphasized in the study of minority group identity. Second, we found that adolescent peers had a lasting influence on Jewish identification for both generations. Third, we revealed a "mild but lasting independent effect" of Jewish education on Jewish identification for the younger generation. This finding appeared at a time when many were questioning the role of formal Jewish education in shaping Jewish identification. Fourth, we found that for younger males, the presence of an older brother was an important independent factor in shaping Jewish identification, a finding not previously emphasized. Fifth, we were able to show, by comparing the patterns of Jewish socialization for a generation of older and younger respondents, that there were some differences that distinguished the two groups. This finding of generational differences suggested that the shaping of Jewish identification is dynamic and that while there are some important and enduring elements, such as the family, other factors may become more important in succeeding generations. For example, Jewish education was one of the factors that was important in the younger generation and not in the older generation.[2]

While we hoped that our book would be reviewed and cited,[3] we did not anticipate that someone would seek to do a replication of our study, as this is rather unusual in the social sciences. Fortunately, one researcher, Alena Janet Strauss, was able to build upon and extend the nature of our study. Since we developed a two-generational analysis which focused on comparing a group of young men between the ages of 22 and 29 to a group of fathers, it was difficult to study comparisons of mothers and daughters due to the frequent name changes after marriage prevalent at that time. Strauss, however, confined her study to 103 young Jewish men and women between the ages of 21 and 29 living in Toronto, Canada. She reported that "there was strong evidence that the two male groups of subjects [hers in Toronto and ours in St. Paul] were alike."[4]

Indeed, Strauss relied upon the questionnaire that we had originally developed and her findings resembled ours. She found a strong similarity between the seven-item measure of our dependent variable of Jewish group identification and her own measure of identification, and suggested that these findings may be replicated in other Jewish communities. Furthermore, she suggested that our measure of Jewish identification utilized for males extends to females as well.

Strauss' results of the analysis of the sources of Jewish identification were similar to ours for the males among her respondents. However, there were some differences that emerged with respect to her female respondents. With respect to males, for example, both Strauss and we found that father's religiosity was the most important variable, followed by friends' expectations, Jewish education, and activities with parents. For females, however, Strauss found activities with parents was the most important, followed by Jewish education, friends' expectations, and father's religiosity. We are most grateful to Alena Janet Strauss for her replication, which suggests that our findings on ethnic identification have some general applicability to North American Jews.

The reissue of our book appears at a time when interest in the experience of American Jews is heightened by the appearance of the 1990 National Jewish Population Survey (NJPS). The results of this survey will be appearing in articles and monographs throughout the current decade. While such a national survey is not likely to provide a detailed analysis of the socialization process in shaping Jewish identification, it can define the parameters of the population within which these experiences occur. In order to situate our analysis of the process of socialization to Jewish identification in the contemporary context of the dynamics of American Jewry, we present seven major findings that have been emphasized by the authors of NJPS:

1. *Population:* The core Jewish population of the United States in 1990 was approximately 5.5 million, which is about the same as it was in 1970. (However, the proportion of Jews in the U.S. has declined from a high of 3.7% in the 1930s to the current level of 2.2%.)

2. *Households:* Only 17% of households containing a core Jew consist of two Jewish parents and their children. The great majority of Jewish households are of some other variety, such as single-parent families, singles, as well as various blended families.

3. *Intermarriage:* In the past two decades, intermarriage has become much more common. Overall, 26% of all households have experienced intermarriage. Since 1985 about one-half of Jews by birth have intermarried.[5]

4. *Children:* About 1.1 million out of 5.5 million Jews in the United States, or 20%, are children under 18.

5. *Social Characteristics:* The Jewish population of the U.S. is highly educated, with about 60% of males and 45% of females having a college education. Furthermore, there is a good deal of residential mobility within the community, with nearly one-half of the population having changed its residence in the last six years.

6. *Anti-Semitism:* While only a small proportion of American Jews has experienced anti-Semitism on the job (5%), the great majority of American Jews (79%) perceive anti-Semitism as a problem.

7. *Jewish Education:* At the time of the study, 400,000 children were receiving a Jewish education, with one-third of them receiving this educa-

tion in an all-day school.[6]

What do these data mean?[7] They suggest that the current Jewish population is remaining stable, but that the variety of household types has shift-
ed away from the traditional pattern. Consequently, the Jewish socialization process has become much more complicated. While boundaries
between Jews and Gentiles have decreased, as evidenced by the rise in
intermarriage, there are still boundaries of which Jews are keenly aware,
such as viewing anti-Semitism as a problem. Of course, the continued
existence of boundaries is necessary for the maintenance of a distinctive
ethnic and religious identity in the absence of externally enforced barriers
in the form of discrimination and racism. The increase in geographic
mobility, however, poses problems for the maintenance of Jewish identification, in that the severing of associational ties to existing communities
disrupts patterns of Jewish identification. These ties take several years to
be re-established. Finally, with respect to the 20% of the population that
are children, we note that a little more than one-third are receiving some
form of Jewish education at the time of the study and, of that population,
one-third of them are in the more intensive form of the day school. This
finding suggests that variations in Jewish educational experience will continue to be an important element in the shaping of Jewish identification,
which is a finding that originally was highlighted in our study.

Naturally, it is for others to determine the impact of a work on their
own personal and professional lives. At least we know that we took our
own findings very seriously in the implications they portended for our
own personal lives, placing a stress on family relations, formal and informal education, and observance of ethical and ritual norms. Our partners in
the process continue to be our spouses, Sandy and Shelly, to whom we
rededicate this book together with our children, Michael and Alisa and
Lynne, Beth and Jill. Finally, we would like to thank J. Alan Winter and
Barry Kosmin for the very helpful comments they provided on an earlier
draft of this preface, and the editorial staff of University Press of America
for their very gracious assistance.

Notes

1. The community under study, St. Paul, Minnesota, has changed
somewhat in the past two decades along some lines identified originally in
our study. According to the campaign director of the local United Jewish
Fund Council, the population has declined from 10,500 Jews in 3,500
households in 1970, to 7,500 people in 3,000 households in 1990.
Regional diffusion of the population has increased and along with it the
emergence of new congregations.

2. One clarification about the discussion of our findings is necessary
with respect to our reference to "structural effects" in Chapter 5 and following. We mean by that term a short-hand for the notion of the individual's integration into the structure of the community.

3. A lot of people let us know what they thought of the book and how

they cited it, and so we would like to thank the many individuals who reviewed our book in the scholarly and popular press for their praise and their criticism.

4. Alena Janet Strauss, *Social Psychological Determinants of Jewish Identification Among Canadians in Their Twenties*, Master's Thesis, University of Toronto, 1979, p. ii.

5. Some scholars have questioned these figures and additional detailed studies will be forthcoming.

6. For more details about the 1990 NJPS, see Barry A. Kosmin, Sidney Goldstein, Joseph Waksberg, Nava Lerer, Ariella Keysar, and Jeffrey Scheckner, *Highlights of the CJF 1990 National Jewish Population Survey*, New York: Council of Jewish Federations, 1991.

7. Scholars have been debating the meaning of empirical measures of the behavior and attitudes of American Jews for several decades. A succinct summary of the opposing optimistic and pessimistic viewpoints respectively appears in Steven M. Cohen and Charles S. Liebman, *The Quality of American Jewish Life—Two Views*, New York: American Jewish Committee, 1987.

Acknowledgments

The idea of writing this book together was first suggested by our adviser in graduate school at the University of Minnesota, Don Martindale. The idea was nurtured by Dan Cooperman, also of the University of Minnesota, who encouraged us to apply our sociological imagination to the study of contemporary American Jewry. The first fruits consisted of our separate doctoral dissertations completed while at Minnesota and a descriptive account, *The Jewish Community of Saint Paul,* coauthored by us after leaving Minnesota and based on data first presented in our respective dissertations.

When we both moved to New England from Minnesota the idea was further cultivated by Murray Straus at the University of New Hampshire, who encouraged us to write this book and pointed out new questions to be answered and fresh insights to be derived from our available data. Particularly helpful in the data-analysis phase were two colleagues at the University of Connecticut: Stephen Sharkey, who served as a research assistant for one summer, and Zvi Namenwirth, who aided us in factor analyzing our Jewish Identification Scale.

It takes careful pruning to produce a final manuscript. We are indebted to Bernard Lazerwitz of the University of Missouri, who carefully read a draft of our monograph and made many useful suggestions, particularly in tightening up our discussion of methodological techniques. Jan Weiner, an undergraudate student at the University of Connecticut, also read the manuscript and offered many helpful comments to improve the readability of the manuscript.

Sociological studies such as this one involve costly research expenditures. We were fortunate to have received financial support for the data-collection phase and the initial stage of data analysis (the St. Paul Jewish Study Project) from the Graduate School of the University of Minnesota, the Family Study Center of the University of Minnesota, and the National Foundation for Jewish Culture. During this phase of the research in Minnesota we received the cooperation of many members of the St. Paul and Minneapolis Jewish communities, both familiar faces and anonymous respondents, which we gratefully acknowledge.

The second phase of our research, from which this book is more immediately derived, was supported by two grants from the University of Connecticut Research Foundation and by Faculty Summer Fellowships received by each of us from our respective Universities of Connecticut and New Hampshire. Rita Goven and Selma Wollman of the typing pool of the University of Connecticut Research Foundation had the difficult task of typing the manuscript in its various stages, and we greatly appreciate their efforts. To all of these persons we express our gratitude; but, of course, we assume responsibility for any errors in the manuscript.

Last, but most dear, we are indebted to our wives, Sandy and Shelley, and to our children, Michael and Alisa and Lynne and Beth, who endured so much so that we might complete this manuscript. Many times we *shlept* them back and forth between Connecticut and New Hampshire so that we could all be together while we were working on our book. At times we felt exasperated in trying to cope with living in one house, and it seemed that the book would be born a bastard. While we all suffered a little, we grew to love each other more. Perhaps that is the most beautiful flower we have planted in our minds and hearts as we complete these words on Jewish Arbor Day.

1 Being Jewish: A Sociological Approach

The sociological analysis of ethnic groups has focused primarily on two issues: intergroup relations (recently in terms of conflict and violence) and prejudice and discrimination. This emphasis is in large part because of the cruelties—indeed, horrors—that have resulted from social life functioning in terms of dominant-minority relations. One does not have to be a sociologist to know about American slavery, the subjugation of American Indians, the Nazi holocaust, the South African apartheid system, or other instances of contemporary racism. These and similar situations have resulted in studying minority groups from the point of view of social problems. The drama and magnitude of many of these events have captured the interests of sociologists as well as others.

The Basis of Ethnic Identification: Positive or Negative?

Our approach, on the other hand, is based on an appreciation of the viability and in some cases exceptional vitality of minority group life. While not trying to glorify the condition of disadvantaged minorities, there are positive aspects of, say, Black-American or Spanish-American life that do not exist within the dominant community. Furthermore, other American minorities have a quality of life that many would consider different but "advantaged" (in terms of higher socioeconomic status and lower crime rates) compared to the general society. The Amish, Mormons, and Jews all fit into this category, although they are in many ways incomparable, particularly in the degree of divergence from the dominant patterns of American society. That minorities have quite positive features for their members and for the society as a whole is only recently being fully recognized by those both within and outside of these groups.

In this study we are concerned with minority group identification—in particular Jewish identification. The traditional approach to group identification has been to focus on intergroup hostility and prejudice and discrimination. According to Rose and Rose, group identification occurs when "the members feel that they are the objects of prejudice and discrimination" (1965: 247). In another place Rose states that "in the United States minority groups develop group identification as an adjustment to, and a way of opposing, majority prejudice" (1965: 684). In the same vein, the authors of

1

probably the most widely used textbook in the sociology of minorities write: "A sense of group identification is, in fact, to a greater or lesser degree an almost universal result of discrimination" (Simpson and Yinger, 1972: 198). This theme is also readily apparent in the sociological literature about American Jewry. Consider the following statement in one of the most recent works on the topic:

These two external factors [Nazism and the establishment of the State of Israel] are indirect influences on Jewish identification and may be overemphasized. A more direct influence is the rejection of Jews by non-Jews in the United States. Jews have not been fully admitted to the American social structure or the social world of the Protestant majority. A number of community studies have repeatedly pointed to the caste-like line between the non-Jewish and Jewish communities in terms of primary group interaction. Even if the social exclusion of the Jew is declining, the fear of discrimination, and concomitant insecurity, may be a powerful factor in the identification of Jews with their own group. (Goldstein and Goldscheider, 1968: 10).

However, the focus on outgroup hostility toward Jewish Americans is certainly not new. *The Ghetto,* Louis Wirth's classic analysis, written in 1928, contains the following passages:

What has held the Jewish community together . . . is . . . the fact that the Jewish community is treated as a community by the world at large. The treatment which the Jews receive at the hands of the press and the general public imposes collective responsibility from without (270).

In the past it was the influx of a constant stream of orthodox Jews that was relied upon to hold the community together and to perpetuate the faith. Today, however, this force can no longer be depended upon. The revival of race prejudice against the Jew has served as a substitute. It has immensely stimulated group consciousness and strengthened solidarity (279).

Outgroup hostility, then, clearly must be considered in the study of Jewish identification. We hope to show that the individual's interpersonal relationships and his position within the social structure must also be carefully considered. These considerations lead us to utilize the sociological approaches of socialization and social structure and personality.

Two premises underlie this study of Jewish identification. First, we believe that much that contributes to the development and maintenance of Jewish identification has a positive communal and individual value. Such factors as a viable Jewish education, positive Jewish experiences with parents and friends during adolescence, and current involvement with other Jews are all important for Jewish identification. Second, we believe that much can be learned about Jewish identification by viewing it in sociological perspective. This entails formulating the concept of identification itself as a sociological phenomenon as well as considering it in terms of such issues as generation, family and peer expectations and activities, parent-child relations, and aspects of one's current social location (religion, class, etc.). Jewish identification is in large part a function of interaction with significant others in primary-group and other reference-group situations. The activities, expectations, and more subtle influences of these others are indispensable to the development of Jewish, or any other, group identification.

The data presented here were collected from members of one community, the Jewish community of St. Paul, Minnesota. While outgroup hostility toward the members of this community has undoubtedly varied over the last fifty years or so, the level of such hostility during the last ten to fifteen years has been consistently low. Variations in Jewish identification, however, do exist; in some cases they are extreme. Even among community members of the same generation who have common historical experiences that include outgroup hostility, these variations exist. Among our respondents Jewish identification is a social psychological variable, and the issues to be discussed and the evidence to be presented will indicate how and why it varies.

The remainder of chapter 1 reviews and analyzes the different uses of the concept of identification and associated concepts. Our own conceptualization of Jewish group identification is presented. Chapter 2 reviews the historical development and contemporary patterns of social organization in the Jewish community where we gathered our data. In chapter 3 we briefly indicate our methods of data collection and present some background information about our respondents. We discuss in some detail the Jewish Identification Scale, since it is the operational measure of the key phenomenon under investigation. The construction of the scale, its validation in terms of personal profile interviews, and the scale's intercorrelations with other Jewish beliefs and attitudes are treated in this chapter. The final section of chapter 3 is devoted to a presentation and analysis of the evidence concerning generational differences in the Jewish Identification Scale and the other Jewish beliefs and attitudes. In chapter 4 we discuss the socialization factors in adolescence that affect Jewish identification in the younger generation. Chapter 5 analyzes the independent contribution that each of our variables makes to the explanation of Jewish identification. Chapter 6 presents a similar analysis for the older generation. Having explored those variables that our emphasis on socialization and social structure lead us to posit as factors in the development and maintenance of Jewish identification, we turn in Chapter 7 to a consideration of a few of the possible consequences of variations in Jewish identification. A discussion of the relationship of Jewish identification to traditional Jewish values, marginality, and intellectuality is presented. Chapter 8 summarizes some of the major issues and findings that have been discussed and considers their implications. Also, in this chapter we depart from our roles as researchers and present some of our own views on Jewish life and Jewish identification. An Appendix presents additional details on the methods employed in the study.

Identity

Identity is probably the most widely used concept to describe the individual's sense of who he is. However, in the many works dealing with identity in general (or Jewish identity in particular), different usages frequently appear. While it is not our intention to review the literature, which has already been done (de Levita, 1965), we will briefly indicate the fundamental usages of identity and its relationship to identification:

Identity may best be understood if it is viewed first as a higher-order concept, i.e., a general organizing referent which includes a number of subsidiary facets. It may be compared to a concept like education on the sociocultural level. Indeed, Parsons (1968: 20) has referred to identity as "the pattern-maintenance code system of the individual personality." (In his terminology pattern-maintenance includes the educational process.) As education is the sector of the sociocultural system that maintains social stability through the production, consumption, and dissemination of knowledge, identity is the sector of the personal system that maintains personal continuity through the coherent organization of information about the individual. Furthermore, as measurement of the educational system must be made in terms of lower-order concepts, i.e., operationally definable and researchable units, such as, literacy rates or level of formal education, so measurements of identity are carried out in terms of self-reported statements or placement in social categories, such as age, sex, and race. (Dashefsky, 1972: 240).

There are two major sources of a person's identity: the social roles that constitute the shared definitions of appropriate behavior, and the individual life history. Both the person and others base their conception of his identity on these two sources. Table 1-1 combines these two dimensions to describe four facets of identity: social identity, self-conception, personal identity, and ego identity.

The concept of *social identity* refers to how others identify the person in terms of broad social categories or attributes, such as age, occupation, or ethnicity, as in the description "middle-aged Jewish lawyer" (Goffman, 1963: 2; Gordon, 1968: 118; McCall and Simmons, 1966: 64). These face-sheet data are easily obtained through initial observation or in survey research. On the other hand, *self-conception* is a cognitive phenomenon which consists of the set of attitudes an individual holds about himself. It has been operationally defined by Kuhn and McPartland through asking respondents to answer the question "Who am I?" Such a technique yields a set of statements about the individual; "I am a Jew" or "I am a husband" or "I am a clothing salesman" (1954). Social identity corresponds to self-conception in that both are based in large part on social roles. In the former, others define appropriate behavior for the individual in such roles, and in the latter, the individual internalizes these definitions to form a part of his self-conception. Frequently in the sociological literature the distinction between identity and self-conception is overlooked. DeLevita has suggested that the self-concept may be viewed as a higher-order concept including such lower-order concepts as self-perception and self-evaluation (1965: 158-64). This is similar to the point we made about the usage of identity. While identity deals with defining who the individual is, self-concept refers to the individual's reflection about his identity.

The concept of *personal identity* refers to how others define the person in terms of a unique combination of traits that come to be attached to him, as in the statement "Harvey is a nice boy: He's good to his mother" (Goffman, 1963: 57; McCall and Simmons 1966: 64). Biographical data and the observation of patterns of behavior provide a way of studying personal identity on the empirical level. By contrast, *ego identity* is an intrapsychic phenomenon that consists of the psychological core of what the person means to himself (Erikson, 1963: 261-62). It is empirically studied through psychiatric or psychoanalytic depth interviews. For instance, Alexander Portnoy seeks professional help in exploring his ego identity when a voluptuous Israeli Jewish woman who reminds him of his mother renders him impotent after several successful love affairs with Gentile women (Roth, 1967). Personal identity corresponds to ego identity in that both are based on the individual's personal experiences. While others' perception of the individual's past experiences determine his personal identity, his ego identity is based on the same experiences as they have affected him.

Our concern, however, deals particularly with identification rather than the more general phenomenon of identity. In what way are they related?

Identification and Ethnic Group Identification

Just as a good deal of semantic confusion surrounds the term *identity*, so also with regard to the term *identification*. As Winch has noted:

There can be no dispute as to the confusion surrounding the term when the user is trying to be precise in his denotation, but if the term is used without qualifiers, it can serve very well to denote not a single variable but a whole area of inquiry. . . . It follows, then, that when an attempt is made to refer to identification as a variable, one or more qualifying words or phrases are required to communicate with precision (1962: 29).

Identity in any one of its facets is built up through a series of identifications. As Erikson has suggested, "Identity thus is not the sum of childhood

Table 1-1
Facets of Identity

| Definition By | Sources of Definition | |
	Social Roles	Individual Life History
Other	Social Identity	Personal Identity
Person	Self Conception	Ego Identity

identifications, but rather a new combination of old and new identification fragments" (1964: 90). Dashefsky has reviewed some of the literature in this regard:

Foote [1952] and Lindesmith and Strauss [1968] have suggested that identification involves linking oneself to others in an organizational sense (as in becoming a formal member of an association) or in a symbolic sense (as in thinking of oneself as a part of a particular group). Stone [1962] argues further that identification subsumes two processes: "identification of" and "identification with." The former involves placing the individual in socially defined categories. This facilitates the occurrence of the latter. In Stone's terms it is "identification with" that gives rise to identity. Finally, Winch [1962: 28] follows this interactionist approach to define identification as "the more or less lasting influence of one person . . . on another"

Rosen has gone further in arguing that an individual may identify himself (herself) with others on three levels [1965: 162-66]: First, one may identify oneself with some important person in one's life, e.g., a parent or a friend (i.e., a significant other). Second, one may identify oneself with a group from which one draws one's values, e.g., family or co-workers (i.e. a reference group). Last, one may identify oneself with a broad category of persons, e.g., an ethnic group or occupational group (i.e., a social category). It is on the third level that ethnic group identification occurs (1972: 242).

Rose and Rose have emphasized that ethnic group identification implies a positive orientation:

It involves not only a recognition that because of one's ancestry one is a member of a racial or religious group, and a recognition that the majority group defines one as belonging to that racial or religious group; it also involves a positive desire to identify oneself as a member of a group and a feeling of pleasure when one does so (1965: 247).

Following this conceptualization, a high degree of ethnic group identification combined with a sense of absolutism (that one's own definition of relatedness to the group is the only right one) produces chauvinism. By contrast a low degree (or absence) or ethnic group identification combined with sense of absolutism produces the phenomenon to which Lewin referred as group self-hatred (1948).

We define *group identification* as a generalized attitude indicative of a personal attachment to the group and a positive orientation toward being a member of the group. Therefore, *ethnic group identification* occurs when the group in question is one with whom the individual believes he has a common ancestry based on shared individual characteristics and/or shared sociocultural experiences. Such groups may be viewed by their members and/or outsiders as religious, racial, national, linguistic, or geographical (Gordon, 1964). In sum, it can be concluded, following Winch (1962), that ethnic identification "is both a *process* as Stone has suggested and a *product* as Rosen has emphasized," (Dashefsky 1972: 242-43).

Jewish Group Identification

In 1970 the Israeli Supreme Court rendered its judgment in the case of Lieutenant Commander Benjamin Shalit. Commander Shalit had sought to register his children as Jews by nationality *but without any religion*. This did not conform to Israeli regulations based on Jewish religious law *(halakhah)*. The children did not meet the criteria of being born to a Jewish mother or one converted to Judaism. The mother, Anne Shalit, was of Scottish and French Christian origin, but the family professed no formal religious beliefs. The ruling handed down by the Court permitted the children to register as Jews by nationality without declaring a religion. Thus, one could be a Jew in Israel if one defined oneself as such in a cultural or national sense even though not defined as one in a religious sense (Roshwald, 1970).

Could this be extended to include a person who considered himself a Jew by nationality, and, for example, a Christian by religion? Such a matter was also brought before the Israeli Supreme Court in the famous Brother Daniel case a few years before the Shalit decision. Oswald Rufeisen was born a Jew in Poland in 1922 and was active in a Zionist youth movement. As he was preparing to emigrate to Palestine, World War II erupted. He was imprisoned twice and escaped twice. While hiding in a monastery he converted to Catholicism and later became a Carmelite monk. Brother Daniel, as he was known in his monastic order, eventually migrated to Israel in 1958 and applied for citizenship under the Law of Return, which grants citizenship virtually automatically to any Jew who settles in Israel. He claimed that he was a Jew by nationality and a Catholic by religion. The ruling of the Supreme Court did not permit him to attain citizenship under the Law of Return, arguing that a Jew who formally converts to another religion severs his ties to Jewry as well as to Judaism. He was, however, allowed to become a naturalized citizen (Roshwald, 1970).

How do these two cases bear on Jewish identity? First, they point out the complexity of defining what it is to be a Jew. Second, they suggest that being a Jew depends on the congruence of one's own definition and that of others. As Sartre (1948) and Eisenstadt (1970) have suggested, a Jew is someone who considers himself to be one and is considered by others to be one. In social psychological terms, as we have pointed out, there is some correspondence between one's social identity and one's self-conception. Third, these cases indicate that Jewish group identification reflects loyalty to the Jewish people, not specifically to its religious precepts, although formally adopting another religion severs the ties of peoplehood. These rulings tend to give juridical support to the linguistic significance of the Hebrew word *Yahadut,* the one word used to stand for both Jewry and Judaism.

A surfeit of terms has gained currency in the study of being Jewish: identity, group identification, identification, consciousness, selfconsciousness, self-conception, etc. The long list can be reduced to the two terms we have discussed: identity and identification. As pointed out earlier, identity involves defining who an individual is on the basis of judgments by oneself and others; and identification, or linking oneself to others, is a process through which identity is established. Out intention here is not to review the varying usages of these terms (see Brodsky, 1968; and Fainstein and Feder, 1966), but rather to suggest how our study relates to the extant literature.

Much of the usage of the terms identification, Jewish consciousness, and self-consciousness (Ben-Yehuda, 1966) has referred to Jewish group idenftication, which deals with how the individual relates to the group. Other terms, such as Jewish identity and self-conception, refer to the subjective importance of being a Jew within the whole range of subidentities and roles to which a person is socialized.

Our concern, however, is with Jewish group identification. Others have dealt with this notion previously, even though they may not have defined it as such. One of the pioneers in this area of research was Lewin, who in several essays helped to bring the study of Jewish group identification to the attention of social scientists. He observed: "It is for example one of the greatest theoretical and practical difficulties of the Jewish problem that Jewish people are often, in a high degree, uncertain of their relation to the Jewish group, in what respect they belong to this group, and in what degree" (1948: 148). Lewin raised the theoretical and practical questions of studying the strength and type of Jewish group identification. Others subsequently sought to study it empirically (Yarrow: 1958; Brenner: 1960; Segalman: 1966; and Rutchik: 1968). Our attempt is to go beyond descriptions of Jewish identification and study some of its determinants.

Summary

We introduce our study of Jewish indentification by contrasting the outgroup hostility approach with our own socialization (and social structure and personality) approach. While prejudice and discrimination toward American Jewry are undoubtedly a factor, we focus on the interpersonal and group experiences within the Jewish community which develop and maintain an individual's Jewish identification.

Since the issue we are dealing with is identification, a part of this chapter is devoted to explicating and clarifying this concept. We do this by introducing the facets of *identity* which define who the individual is. These concepts are contrasted with *identification,* which is used to describe an individual's attachments to others. Identification is a social psychological mechanism through which identity is formed and changed. Chapter 1, then, introduces the topic and provides the preliminary conceptual underpinning for our investigation of the sources and concomitants of Jewish group identification.

Our working definition of Jewish (group) identification is based on our discussion of ethnic (group) identification. *Jewish identification* is a generalized attitude indicative of a personal attachment to the Jewish people. The preceding discussion sets the stage for our investigation of some of the sources of Jewish identification among American Jews in one community.

2

The Jewish Community of Saint Paul: Historical and Contemporary Patterns

Two centuries ago, the question of who was a Jew in the Western world could easily be answered by ascertaining who observed Jewish law. Today, however, the trends of nationalism, rationalism, secularism, and pluralism, which have been accelerating in many societies since the French Revolution, have fragmented the once fairly uniform definition of a Jew. These trends provided the backdrop for the Israeli controversy referred to as the Shalit Affair, in which an Israeli Jew sought to register his children as Jews by virtue of national ties even though they failed to meet the criteria of Jewish religious law *(halakhah)*.

The successive Jewish migrations to the United States of Sephardim in the colonial period, of Germans in the nineteenth century, and East Europeans from 1880 through the 1920s produced changes in American Jewish life. The Orthodoxy transported from the old country was modified by some to fit the American experience and was completely abandoned by others for the liberal interpretation of German-based Reform Judaism. The latter offered the earlier immigrant Jews a greater opportunity to assimilate into American culture and to maintain their newly acquired prestige and social position, which were threatened by the large influx of Orthodox Eastern European refugees and immigrants arriving in the late nineteenth century.

Conservative Judaism arose as an American response at the turn of the twentieth century. Marshall Sklare has summarized it best:

Conservatism mediates between the demands of the Jewish tradition, the feeling of both alienation and nostalgia toward first and second settlement areas, and the norms of middle-class worship. In effect it borrows something from each of these elements and synthesizes them into a new pattern (1972: 376).

In an attempt to deal with the apparently irresistible trends referred to earlier, Reconstructionist Judaism developed in the middle of the twentieth century. It proposed a reconstruction of Judaism that conceived it as a religious civilization in which religion (without supernaturalism) was central but represented only one aspect of Jewish life. While to date only a small proportion of American Jews even know what Reconstructionism is, it is our contention that Reconstructionist principles, nevertheless, are a basic part of the American Jewish ideology (see chapter 3).

The development of these religious differences reflects new collective

is occasioned by shifts in socioeconomic position and ethnic con-
~~~~. while there presently are differences in attitudes and actions of Jews
adhering to the varying interpretations of Judaism, religious differences
appear to be in large part a function of generation.

A Brief Social History of the Saint Paul Jewish Community[1]

In the early 1820s migrants from the East established the first permanent
settlement in the vicinity of St. Paul near Fort Snelling, which was constructed in 1819. The number of settlers grew very slowly in the first few
decades. After the first land sale, however, immigration from the East
increased significantly. In 1849 the area was organized by Congress as the
Minnesota Territory.

The Early Community (1850-80)[2]   Political organizations

The first Jews arrived in St. Paul in the late 1840s. They were involved in
peddling, trading, and retailing. In 1851 the editor of the St. Paul newspaper
noted that there were a "sprinkling of Jews" in the area. The total population of St. Paul at this time was about one thousand.

   The 1850s were years of much more rapid growth. Most of the new
settlers came from the Middle Atlantic states. A minority came directly
from Europe, primarily from Germany and Scandinavian countries. Jews
participated in this movement to St. Paul. Like the others, most of them had
emigrated to this country (from Germany) and had lived in Eastern states.
Many had accumulated enough capital while in the East to establish
businesses (largely clothing and soft goods) upon arriving in St. Paul.

   By the mid 1850s the Jews of St. Paul had formed a religious organization. In 1856, two years before Minnesota became a state, they organized
the Mt. Zion Hebrew Association, and the following year received their
charter from the territorial government. The establishment of a Jewish
cemetery by this organization made it important for Jews throughout the
area. The religious services and ritual prescriptions of Mt. Zion were
strictly Orthodox in the early years. During the next fifteen years the
members prospered and had excellent relations with their non-Jewish
fellow St. Paulites: According to Plaut, Jews were not excluded anywhere
(1959:53). In 1871 a synagogue built by the Mt. Zion congregation was
dedicated.

   The 1870s saw the arrival of Jewish immigrants to St. Paul who had a
quite different cultural background than their predecessors. They were
Jews of East European origin whose mother tongue was Yiddish. These

new settlers were all referred to as "Polish" by the older members of the Jewish community. However, new German-born immigrants were accepted as family by the older Jewish residents. The East Europeans found the culture of the established St. Paul Jewish community alien and the people unfriendly. They reacted by developing a social life of their own (Plaut, 1959:55). These founders of the "second" Jewish community were not refugees but immigrants who had come to St. Paul for much the same motives as the German Jews.

As has been noted, Mt. Zion was a strictly Orthodox congregation in its early years. However, their Hebrew pronunciation and certain aspects of worship were quite different from that to which the East Europeans were accustomed. In 1872, members of the East European Jewish community, the "Polish" Jews, founded the Sons of Jacob congregation. This organization was incorporated in 1875. The Sons of Jacob established the second Jewish cemetery in the state. By the early 1870s, therefore, there were two congregations and two webs of social relations based on Old Country origins (1959:57).

At this time the Mt. Zion congregation began to move away from its Orthodox position and to lean towards Reform. According to Plaut, there were three general reasons for this. First, the German Jews came from, and established in St. Paul, a liberal intellectual climate. They desired to be both Jews and Americans and felt constrained in fulfilling this desire by Orthodox decrees and practices. Second, these Jews were pioneers in a new territory and, therefore, adept at making adjustments. They were used to changing old ways to fit new conditions. Third, they felt an all the more urgent need to change from the traditional Jewish practices when the East European Jews began to arrive. Although the East Europeans had a decidedly different culture with different language and different dress, the non-Jewish community had not made a definite distinction among St. Paul Jews. To evidence a distinction between themselves and the East Europeans, the Mt. Zion congregation moved into the Reform sphere. Reform was of course unacceptable to most East Europeans Jews, who had always lived a traditionally Jewish life. The reason for the German Jews' desire to maintain a distinction between themselves and the East Europeans was, at least in part, that they felt a qualitative difference, especially culturally, between the two groups.

The 1870s saw the founding of other German-Jewish organizations: the Hebrew Ladies Benevolent Society (primarily a charitable society) in 1871 and the Standard Club in 1875. Of this last organization, Plaut writes: "A social club was established which provided Jews with a suitable and congenial environment of their own, and provided its 'German' members at the same instant with an opportunity to draw intra-Jewish social lines" (1959:59).

During this early period relations between the Jewish community and the non-Jewish community were extremely good. For example, in 1871 the question of Bible reading in the public schools was dropped, with explicit regard for the feelings of the local Jewish populace (1959:85). As another example, when the Mt. Zion congregation announced plans in 1881 to build a new synagogue, it received a number of contributions to its building fund from non-Jewish St. Paulites. Plaut cites four reasons for the friendliness of Jewish-Gentile relations during this period. First, the German Jews shared the same culture as the large number of non-Jewish Germans that had settled in St. Paul; they were therefore able to fully participate in the general community life of St. Paul. Second, Jews had come early to St. Paul and participated in this community before there was any exclusion. Third, it was the German Jews who represented the Jewish community. As well as being culturally homogeneous, other factors made them very acceptable to their non-Jewish peers. These Jews represented the pioneer tradition and established wealth. They were prestigious members of the general community. Furthermore, they were not ghettoized and lived throughout the community of St. Paul. Fourth, owing to intermarriage, many non-Jewish families had one or more Jewish members.

In general, the period of the St. Paul Jewish community's beginning and early years, from around 1850 to 1880, was a period of growth and development. However, even during these years the incipient cleavage was becoming evident.

Immigration and Two Communities (1880-1930)

A wave of persecution of Jews spread over Eastern Europe starting at the beginning of the 1880s. This was not subtle prejudice or mere denial of equal rights; it was the beginning of physical persecution. The Jews of these countries literally feared for their lives. This situation brought hundreds of refugees to St. Paul in 1882, the vanguard of thousands of Jews who would come to St. Paul during the next five decades. Plaut cited three changes in the Jewish community as a consequence of this immigration:

1. There was now a Jewish social welfare problem, which grew in proportion as other immigrants kept coming year after year.
2. There was now a community of far greater complexity, which demanded and created new institutions.
3. The new immigrants formed in effect a community of their own which absorbed the older Jewish settlers of East European background, and this new community would for the next generation develop parallel to that of the German group (1959:95).

The immigration, which lasted into the 1920s, brought Jews from Russia, Poland, Lithuania, Rumania, and other East European countries into St. Paul. These immigrants and many of their East European predecessors formed a second Jewish community in St. Paul much larger than the German community. The separation of St. Paul Jews into two communities was sharp and decisive. It held for almost every aspect of social life. The only area in which the two communities had extensive social relations was welfare. Here the relationship was one way; the German community aided members of the newer East European community. Plaut claimed: "In time, this division was accepted as natural. It was a mutual separation; for the cultural, social and religious interests of the two groups appeared to be incompatible" (1959:110). The separation of the two communities was also physical, with the area of St. Paul known as the West Side (the southern portion of St. Paul, which is on the *west* bank of the Mississippi River) inhabited by the East European community, while the German Jews were primarily concentrated in the more central part of the city. The immigrant Jews lived, as far as possible, the traditionally Jewish lives they had known in the old country. They developed a whole range of institutions, including their *Landsmannschaft* synagogues, on the East European model.

The original part of the West Side to be settled as the East European Jewish community was also called the "flats." According to Hoffman the boundaries of this area were: the river and the city dump, the "West Side Hills" across the State Street Bridge; Robert Street; and another loop of the river (1957:57). This area, close to downtown St. Paul, was the crowded quarters of Jewish immigrant life. It was the first Jewish ghetto area in the city. Within or close to it were the garment and hat factories that employed many of the community's men. Here too were the small and large shops owned by Jews and employing Jews. Others made their living as peddlers: selling fruits and vegetables, household items, or trading in rags. The social life also existed almost entirely on the West Side. Within the community were the synagogues, settlement houses, and social and political organizations. Many of these organizations were patterned after Old World institutions. Even within this community there were divisions. The *Landsmannschaften* (insurance and social organizations) were separated according to the East European national origin of the members. The Yiddish language, however, served as a cohesive force. It was spoken in the home and wherever members of the community congregated.

The effect of this community on the German Jews in St. Paul was strong and direct. The Mt. Zion congregation became radically Reform. Accordingly, its members sought to differentiate themselves from other synagogues in the Jewish community. In 1922 a lay official of Mt. Zion wrote in the Twin Cities' Jewish weekly:

The personnel of the membership of the Congregation has been and is high, and numbers many of the leading merchants and professional men of the community who have been active in the development of the city and of the commonwealth itself. To them, as well as to the spiritual leaders of the congregation, is due the prestige and standing of the congregation (Hess, 1922:39).

By the early 1880s two East European congregations were in existence: the Sons of Jacob, and a newer Russian immigrant congregation, the Sons of Zion. By the turn of the century these congregations had built impressive synagogues, and at least four other Orthodox congregations had made their appearance on the West Side. Hoffman recounts how they came into existence:

The first synagogue services were held in Mr. Rutchik's Hay and Feed store on State and Alabama. Gradually splinter groups left to form their own congregations with the Litvaks and Russians worshipping in separate buildings. The congregation meeting in Rutchik's store subsequently built and occupied the beautiful B'nai Zion Synagogue (1957:57).

By the turn of the century the West Side community had a multifaceted and rich culture. A variety of associations, such as the Free Sons of Israel, B'rith Abraham, Sons of Benjamin, Progressive Order of the West, the Bund, and the Workmen's Circle, served the community's social and intellectual needs. Zionist associations, such as the Young Zionists and Tefereth Zion, also attracted members. Plaut observed: "In response to [the community's] needs a multitude of groups of all sorts had sprung up—so many indeed that they could not possibly continue side by side" (1959:180).

From the very moment that they arrived most immigrants were concerned that their children receive a Jewish education. Hoffman describes this educational process as it existed on the West Side.

The first formal Jewish education was provided in Mr. Bromberg's "chedar" on State and Texas Street before that institution of higher learning—The Talmud Torah—was built. Every Jewish child received a Jewish education generally in an informal way from peddlers who were peddlers out of sheer necessity but scholars at heart. When the long day of work was over, they invited their reluctant scholars to impart Torah and wisdom (1957:22).

Before the turn of the century some members of the West Side community established what was later to become the Capitol City Hebrew School (Greenberg, 1937:33). This school carried on the Old World traditions of the East European Jewish community. It taught Orthodox observance and utilized traditional teaching techniques (Plaut, 1959:175). The first classes were held in the Sons of Abraham building, an Orthodox synagogue. In 1912 a building was purchased to house what was by then the Capitol City Hebrew School.

Another important educational institution of the West Side at the beginning of the century was the Neighborhood House. This institution had been organized some years before as an industrial school in conjunction with the Mt. Zion Hebrew Ladies Benevolent Society. It offered classes in such skills as mending and repairing. By 1900 the school had become Neighborhood House, and in a few years it was serving the entire West Side community on a nonsectarian basis.

In the early 1900s, while the West Side community was still growing, a number of German and East European Jews made their homes in other parts of the city. Some of the earlier East European Jewish residents were solidly middle class with an active interest in the social and economic life of the general St. Paul community, and they moved toward Capitol Hill, near the older German section of the city. The highest status Jews were those from central Europe, mostly German-speaking, who referred to themselves as *Deutsche Yehudim*. They were moving from the Capitol Hill area west. Meanwhile movement was also taking place within the West Side community itself. The first movement was from the "flats" to an adjacent area known as the West Side Hills. The "flats" referred to the area's proximity to the river, and Hoffman tells of homes being soaked with water because of this location. Therefore, the move to higher land in the Hills area was an important step upward for the hard-working immigrant families. The West Side remained the largest Jewish area in St. Paul until the 1920s.

The first two decades of this century were the period of the greatest growth of population in the St. Paul Jewish community (see table 2-1). This was still the time of two separate Jewish Communities, and it was, of course, the East European Jewish community that grew, as Jews from that part of Europe came in vast numbers to this country.

In general, during this period the Jews of St. Paul were improving themselves financially. Calmenson noted that St. Paul had seven or eight Jewish millionaires, and so St. Paul was reputed to have a very wealthy Jewish community (1937:77). Residential movement of St. Paul's Jews also indicated economic progress. While many still lived on the West Side, those in the upper socioeconomic levels lived in the Capitol Hill district (Cohen: 1952:7).

Movement to areas of less dense Jewish settlement, which was accompanied by increased acculturation, set the stage in St. Paul for the development of Conservative Judaism. Unlike Reform and Orthodox Judaism, which were imported from Europe, the Conservative movement was a product of the American experience. It sought to conserve aspects of traditional Jewish living adapted to a secular, yet Christian society. In 1912 the Conservative Temple of Aaron was founded and in 1916 it built its own synagogue. Soon after, the congregation acquired a cemetery. The services of the congregation used the traditional Hebrew liturgy, but sermons and some prayers were given in English. The members were primarily younger men and women (Kleinman, 1922:40).

In the same year that its synagogue building was completed, the Temple

Table 2-1
Population of City of St. Paul, Ramsey County, and Jewish Community and Corresponding Proportion of Jews in City and County for 1800, 1900-1970.

	Population			Proportion of Jews (Percent)	
	City of St. Paul[a]	Ramsey County[a]	Jewish Community*	City of St. Paul	Ramsey County
1880	41,473		225[b]	0.5	
1900	163,065		3,500[c]	2.1	
1910	214,744		5,904[d]	2.8	
1920	234,698		10,000[e]	4.3	
1930	271,606	286,721	13,500[f]	5.0	4.7
1940	287,736	309,935	14,000[g]	4.9	4.5
1950	311,349	355,332	12,000[h]	3.8	3.4
1960	313,411	422,525	10,200[i]	3.2	2.4
1970	308,686[j]	474,823[j]	10,500[k]	3.4	2.2

*The population resides almost entirely within the city.

Sources:

[a]U.S. Census.

[b]*American Jewish Yearbook*, 43, 1941: Estimate for 1877.

[c]*Ibid.*, Estimate for 1905.

[d]U.S. Census, Number of Yiddish-Speaking persons.

[e]*American Jewish Yearbook*, 25, 1923: Estimate for 1917.

[f]Ibid., 32, 1930: Estimate for 1927.

[g]Ibid., 43. 1941: Estimate for 1937.

[h]Ibid., 50, 1949: Estimate for 1948.

[i]Ibid., 62, 1961: Estimate for 1960.

[j]Preliminary U.S. Census figures, 1970.

[k]Estimate for 1968 of United Jewish Fund and Council, St. Paul, including the nearby suburbs.

of Aaron congregation established its own Hebrew School. In 1919 it adopted the *Ivrit B'Ivrit* method of Hebrew instruction (a modern approach for that era employing oral-aural techniques, literally "Hebrew in Hebrew"), and classes were held five days a week. In 1924 the school had an enrollment of one hundred and seventy-five students with five teachers. In 1927 it was made an independent institution (the Center Hebrew School), although it was still housed in the Temple of Aaron building (Gordon, 1957:33). In contrast to this school the Capitol City Hebrew School maintained its affiliation with Orthodoxy. The Hebrew Institute and Sheltering Home also followed a traditional approach to instruction and observance (Greenberg, 1922:45).

Makiesky noted the following changes in the West Side during the first two decades of this century:

Improvement of conditions of all sidewalks and streets. Erection of synagogues and public schools in various parts of the district. Establishment of recreational centers. Expansion of businesses and inception of others. Modernization of homes. Installation of new sewer and waterworks systems. Increase in population.

The dilapidated boards which served as sidewalks are no more— but have been supplanted by white stone walks. And the rugged streets, dotted with refuse and mudpuddles, which made it almost impossible for any vehicle to pass over them, have given way to the smooth bitulithic pavement.

The shabby grocery stores and butcher shops, which were tucked away in small corners of homes and buildings, have vanished, and large up-to-date grocery establishments, butcher shops, dry goods stores, soft drink and confectionary parlors, movie houses, and drug stores have sprung up (1922:55).

By 1922 the many small *shuln* (Yiddish for synagogues, especially traditional East European) on the West Side had been replaced by five Orthodox synagogues: the Agudas Achim Synagogue, the Chevre Mishna Ashkanas Synagogue, the Sons of Israel congregation, the Beth David synagogue, and the Sons of Zion. They served an estimated 3500 members of the St. Paul Jewish community, those who still resided on the West Side.

Up until this point the discussion has been of the two Jewish communities of St. Paul. Even in the early part of this century, however, there were events that pointed to the eventual unification of St. Paul Jewry into one community. One of the first such movements was the opening of the B'nai Brith lodge to East European Jews in the early 1900s. The second impetus in this direction was the Zionist movement. In the 1900s Jews of all backgrounds participated together in this effort. In addition, such unhappy events as the rise of the Ku Klux Klan, with its virulent form of anti-Semitism and the plight of European Jews prevented from immigration by restrictive laws during and after World War I brought all the members of the community closer together (Mackay, 1952:11).

With immigration ending, the community began to stabilize in population. In the 1920s there were over 10,000 Jews in St. Paul, the majority of them of East European origin. The socioeconomic position of this majority continued to rise, so that by 1927 only 31 percent of the Jewish population lived on the West Side (Mackay, 1962:13).

The German Jewish community had been an integral part of the general St. Paul community. Its members were active in the political, economic, and civic life of the city. They belonged to a number of social clubs and held high offices in civic organizations. They were active in the vital banking and heavy industry of the city. However, the great influx of East European Jews with their different culture, coupled with the rising nativist movement, changed this situation markedly:

By 1921, there were rigid social distinctions which divided the bulk of the Jewish population from its Gentile neighbors. There were wide business and employment opportunities which were closed to the Jews, and the attention given to antidefamation by the local representatives of the defense organizations was proof of the existence as well as of their awareness of the problem (Plaut, 1959:200)

This period of great growth, therefore, closed with the end of immigration, the rise of anti-Semitism, and the Depression. Nevertheless, the period from 1880 to 1930 was a dynamic and vital time in the history of the St. Paul Jewish community (Cohen, 1952:7).

Transition and the Emergence of One Community (1930-54)

By 1930 the period of rapid population growth had come to an end. The community did grow moderately during the next ten years, but after 1940 there appears to have been a steady decrease in the proportion of Jews in the total population (see table 2-1). The period between 1930 and 1954 was highlighted by the unification of the community and continued changes in the main areas of residence.

Organizational consolidation played an important part in the community's unification. An initial step in this direction was the opening in 1930 of a Jewish Center at Holly and Grotto. In 1932 the Council of Jewish Social Agencies was formed to facilitate cooperation among organizations devoted to communal welfare (Calmenson, 1937:77). Moreover, in 1934 the Jewish Center formed three separate organizations: an educational association, an activities association, and a Hebrew School association (originally operated by the Temple of Aaron). Another very important event for the unification of the community was the formation of the United Jewish Fund in 1935, which later merged with the Council of Jewish Social Agencies to form the United Jewish Fund and Council. The need in the immediately succeeding years to raise large amounts of money to provide aid for Jews overseas strengthened the position of the United Jewish Fund and Council in the community (Cohen, 1952:7).

The effects of anti-Semitism in the thirties and the realization of what had happened in World War II gave St. Paul Jews much more than common organizations. They felt a strong sense of kinship and a common fate. Neither Hitler nor the anti-Semites in this country discriminated among Jews, and the members of the St. Paul Jewish community fully realized this. Common fears and interests and the massive effort to help relieve the Jewish suffering caused by World War II, helped the St. Paul Jewish community enter the fifties as one community.

The movement to the Hill district was already well advanced by World War II. The movement continued west of Capitol Hill, and a major area of Jewish settlement became known as the Holly-Grotto area. This neighborhood was primarily a transitional area in the community's development, with the next major movement occurring southwest to the Highland Park area. The twenty-five years from 1930 to 1954 were a time of rapid residential movement and organizational, social, and cultural unification for the community.

The Contemporary Community (1954 and After)

The contemporary physical and social pattern of the St. Paul Jewish community emerged, in large part, during the fifties and sixties. Although the Orthodox Sons of Jacob congregation broke ground for an addition in 1952, it was apparent by that time that the Orthodox synagogues were rapidly decreasing in number and size. Both the Reform and Conservative congregations, on the other hand, emerged as major forces in the life of the contemporary community. In 1954 a new synagogue for the Mt. Zion Temple congregation was dedicated; in 1956 a new Temple of Aaron synagogue was dedicated on a site along the Mississippi River. By local standards both of these buildings were impressive as houses of worship and community centers. In the late 1960s the size of the Reform congregation, Mt. Zion, was remaining stable and the membership upper-middle class. The Conservative congregation, Temple of Aaron, was constantly increasing in numbers. Furthermore, the mean age of the members of this congregation had decreased gradually over the years from about fifty-five to about forty. (For synagogue membership figures, see table 2-3).

In 1964 a new Jewish Community Center building was opened in Highland Park. Along with the major congregations, this organization provided the recreational centers for the St. Paul Jewish community. They also provided adult education courses on Jewish subjects. The primary institution for the Jewish education of the young, however, remained the Talmud Torah.

By the late sixties, the great majority of St. Paul's Jews resided in Highland Park. The investments in this area both in homes and community buildings would seem to indicate Highland Park as the physical base of the Jewish community for the foreseeable future. An increasing but still small number of families, particularly among the younger generation, appeared to be moving south across the Mississippi River to suburban Mendota Heights.

According to some Jewish leaders in St. Paul, the pattern of residence and population was a problem for the community. They believed that St. Paul was losing its young people, and the Jewish community disproportionately so, because their young adults were more highly mobile. This loss was attributed to geographical and economic factors: the river cuts the city off in the south precisely where the Jewish community is located (figure 2-1), and St. Paul was said to be losing much of its industry.

Another problem that the community began to face during this period

22

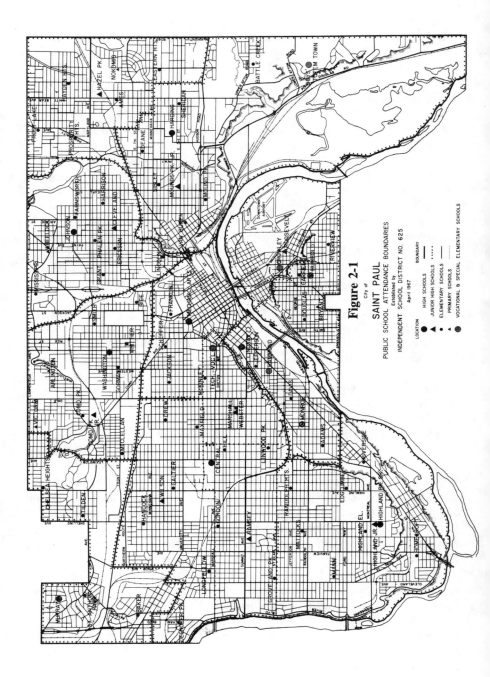

Figure 2-1

City of

SAINT PAUL

PUBLIC SCHOOL ATTENDANCE BOUNDARIES

Established by

INDEPENDENT SCHOOL DISTRICT NO. 625

April 1967

LOCATION

● HIGH SCHOOLS — BOUNDARY ——
▲ JUNIOR HIGH SCHOOLS ·····
● ELEMENTARY SCHOOLS ——
● PRIMARY SCHOOLS ········
● VOCATIONAL & SPECIAL ELEMENTARY SCHOOLS

was its relationship with the disadvantaged in St. Paul. Mt. Zion Temple had a social action program and housed two Head Start programs. The Jewish Family Service handled many cases of non-Jewish disadvantaged families. Nevertheless, there was apparent friction between individual Jews and blacks in St. Paul, particularly where there was economic contact and/or residential propinquity.

Another concern during this period was the threat to Israel's survival occasioned by the Six Day War in June of 1967. The unified action and fund raising during this crisis indicated the extent to which the St. Paul Jewish community was unified and capable of a powerful and effective response.

While the history of the community becomes in varying ways a part of each person's experience, the current organization and activity of the community is the contemporary reality that constitutes part of the social base of the individual's Jewish identity. We, therefore, turn to a description of that reality.

The Social Organization of Saint Paul Jewry[3]

By the 1960s, Highland Park had become equated with the St. Paul Jewish community. The United Jewish Fund and Council estimated that in 1968, 80 percent of the Jews in St. Paul were Highland Park residents. Despite the heavy concentration of Jews in this area, it was still predominantly non-Jewish.

The Locale

Areas of Jewish residential concentration during the period 1954-68 can be inferred from the enrollment figures of male Jewish seniors in St. Paul high schools (table 2-2). Figure 2-1 shows the locations and attendance boundaries of all of St. Paul's public schools.

In each year the overwhelming majority of male Jewish high school seniors were concentrated in one school. Central High School served the entire southwestern portion of the city until the opening of Highland Park Senior High in 1964. By 1968, nine out of ten students in the above category attended the new high school. Thus, on the basis of public high school attendance in 1968 the Jews of St. Paul were located in the area bordered by Summit Avenue on the north, the Mississippi River on the south and west, and Lexington Avenue on the east.

Data on Talmud Torah enrollment in 1967 indicated a similar pattern. Secondary school students represented 40 percent of the total enrollment. Thirty-three percent of the total enrollment attended Highland Park Junior

Table 2-2
Male Jewish Seniors in St. Paul Area High Schools
(Percent)

	Year	
School	1954 [a]	1968
Central	76	5
Highland Park Senior		87
Humboldt	8	1
Marshall [b]	5	
Mechanic Arts	6	
Sibley (West St. Paul) [c]		4
Other	4	3
TOTAL	99 [d]	100
	(N=80)	(N=151)

Source: High-school data were made available through the Student Counseling Bureau of the University of Minnesota.
Note: The much greater number of seniors in 1968 (151) than in 1954 (80) reflects the demographic effects of World War II.
[a] In 1954 juniors completed a form that included the information on religion.
[b] No longer had senior high school students.
[c] School located in southern suburbs (not shown on map).
[d] Error due to rounding.

and Senior Highs and 7 percent attended other secondary schools. In other words, more than eight out of ten secondary school students enrolled in the Talmud Torah lived in Highland Park. Moreover, the enrollment of elementary school students in the Talmud Torah allows us to infer more specifically the primary area of Jewish residence. Fifty-nine percent of all Talmud Torah students were in elementary school. Of the total enrollment 15 percent attended Highland; 17 percent Homecroft; and 10 percent Mann. This meant that seven out of every ten elementary school students enrolled in the Talmud Torah lived within: Randolph Avenue on the north, Snelling Avenue on the east, and the Mississippi River on the south and west. Despite the fact that not all Jewish children of St. Paul attended the Talmud Torah, the residential distribution of its students was similar to that of Jewish male high school seniors.

Population

The growth of the Jewish community did not keep pace with the population growth of St. Paul (table 2-1). The proportion of Jews rose from 0.5 percent to 5 percent during the period 1880 to 1930, while the actual number of Jews increased sixtyfold. In the decade of the Depression the number of Jews peaked at about 14,000 people and began to decline. This decrease, though not as rapid as the increase in the earlier phase of the community's development, continued until 1960, when the number of Jews in the city dropped to 10,200.

This figure remained fairly constant over the decade of the 1960s, with an estimated 3.4 percent of the city's population being Jewish. The percentage of residents of Greater St. Paul (Ramsey County) who were Jewish, however, declined from 3.4 in 1950 to 2.2 in 1970. These latter figures indicated more accurately the size of the Jewish community vis-á-vis the larger community.

It was estimated that the 10,500 Jews living in St. Paul in 1970 constituted about 3500 family units, with an average family size of 3.0. The national Jewish average was 3.2, but St. Paul had a disproportionate number of older Jewish families.[4]

The testimony of several community leaders indicated that the emigration that was taking place involved young people in their twenties who were moving to Minneapolis and other communities. The loss of these young people in their "productive" and child-bearing years hindered the continued growth of the community.

Social Stratification

There do not appear to be any great differences in life styles on the basis of socioeconomic status in this community. As in any community, however, there were those who by virtue of their financial position were able to spend their leisure time in certain activities such as country club participation and vacations abroad and in resort areas. These activities were pursued by the community's social "elite."

The majority of the Jews of St. Paul, however, belonged to the broad middle stratum of the community, the "less elite," who were relatively affluent, but who did not participate in certain leisure activities. At the bottom of the socioeconomic ladder was a small group, the "nonelite," who were distinguished by their lack of affluence. They included for the most part older elements of the population engaged in manual labor, lower-level sales and clerical occupations, and some small businessmen. The elite and less elite included individuals who were engaged in business or professional careers. Among the younger elements of the population there was a shift from more traditional Jewish occupations of entrepreneurs and independent professionals to careers in the bureaucratized professions of business, industry, and education.

Community Decision Making

The strongest single base of decision making was the United Jewish Fund and Council, the community's central charitable fund. While the Fund made decisions for local collection and disbursement of money, quotas for Israel and overseas causes were established nationally.

Other centers of community decision making existed within the various organizations and associations. The most powerful ones were within the larger synagogues (particularly the Conservative and Reform temples). Each combined mass membership with group solidarity, fostered by organizational and interpersonal involvement and ideological attachment. This facilitated their role in community decision making. In these organizations the decisions were made through the cooperation of the lay and professional leadership, the rabbi being the most important figure. Within most Jewish organizations the professional executive director (or his equivalent), because of his experience and knowledge, was often able to guide the decisions of the lay leaders, especially if he had been in his position for a long time. The cooperation of lay and professional leaders permitted interorganizational unity on urgent matters, such as support for Israel before and after the Six Day War.

The Fund and synagogue leadership, by virtue of some overlapping membership and through effective informal communication, constituted the St. Paul Jewish community's decision-making center. It was able to operate most efficiently, however, only during crisis situations when individuals tended to overlook the differences that often separated them and were more susceptible to compromise and concerted action.

Synagogue and Temple

The fundamental occurrence in the community's organized religious life was the decline of membership in Orthodox synagogues. A listing of the Jewish organizations in St. Paul in 1900 showed that the five Orthodox congregations had a combined membership of 370 and the one Reform congregation (Mt. Zion) had only 107 members.[5] Thus, over three-quarters of the members of synagogues belonged to Orthodox congregations. Nearly seventy years later in 1968 there were still five Orthodox congregations (though not, except in one instance, the same ones). However, while their combined membership had increased, the *proportion* of total Orthodox synagogue members had *decreased* to less than one quarter. The Reform synagogue had also gained members, but its proportion of the total synagogue membership had risen only to slightly more than one quarter. The prime beneficiary of this shift away from Orthodox synagogue affiliation was the one Conservative synagogue (Temple of Aaron). It claimed nearly half the total synagogue members in 1968 (table 2-3). One of the largest categories in table 2-3 is those individuals who did not belong to any

Table 2-3.
Family Synagogue Membership (1968)

Name of Synagogue and Type	Number of Synagogue-Affiliated Families	Percent of Synagogue-Affiliated Families	Percent of All Jewish Families
Mount Zion (Reform)	750	29	21
Temple of Aaron (Conservative)	1250	48	36
Sons of Jacob (Orthodox)	275	11	8
Adath Israel (Orthodox)	75	3	2
Gedaliah Leib (Orthodox)	150	6	4
Beth Israel (Orthodox)	50	2	1
Highland Park Minyan (Orthodox)[a]	50	2	1
Orthodox Subtotal	600	24	16
Synagogue Subtotal	2600		73
Non-Synagogue Family Units[b]	900		26
Grand Total	3500	101[c]	99[c]

Source: Estimates made by officials of each synagogue.

[a]Temporary congregation met in rented quarters for High Holiday services in 1968.

[b]Estimate derived by subtracting total synagogue family units from estimated total Jewish family units (supplied by United Jewish Fund and Council, St. Paul)

[c]Error due to rounding.

synagogue; in 1968 they represented an estimated one-quarter of the total Jewish population.

The image of the synagogue as a house of worship and study applied more so to the smaller Orthodox congregations. It appeared that as the synagogue increased in size and wealth, it became the setting for other activities of a recreational or cultural nature, a house of congregation. This applied to all three types of synagogues in St. Paul, though to varying degrees.

The rabbinic leadership of the Orthodox synagogues have kept faith with the notion of *Torah MiSinai* (divine revelation) and have encouraged their members to carefully observe the ritual commandments. The rabbinic leadership of the Conservative and Reform temples have emphasized instead various innovations and modifications in the tradition (differing in form and content from one another, with the former adhering more to the tradition than the latter).

School and Shul

Jewish education in both St. Paul and Minneapolis retained a feature fairly uncommon among American Jewish communities: the operation of a central communal afternoon school, the Talmud Torah. While in most cities the synagogues have come to dominate Jewish educational activities, in St. Paul the Talmud Torah continued (as in its twin city of Minneapolis) to be the central Jewish school.

This school combined progressive educational methods with a fairly traditional curriculum, including study of the Hebrew language, Bible, Jewish history, and Jewish customs and ceremonies. Its enrollment rose during 1950-63 from about 300 to 550. Nevertheless, in the ensuing five years the enrollment decreased to approximately 450 in 1968. School sources, who provided these figures, speculated that the decline occurred because of a decreasing birth rate and the out-migration of young Jewish families.

A comparison of the enrollment in the Talmud Torah for 1952 and 1967 (years for which data were available) supported in part the above observation. School-age children in the first through third grades represented 66 percent of the total enrollment in 1952; in contrast, these same grades in 1967 represented only 44 percent of the total enrollment. The greater proportion of older children was met with an expanded secondary-level program. Nevertheless, there were still more children enrolled in 1967 in grades 1-3 (203) than in 1952 (190). If the Jewish population of St. Paul, however, continues to decline, particularly in the age cohort of the twenties, these three grades of younger children will fall below the 1952 figure.

In addition to the Talmud Torah, several synagogue schools provided training oriented towards their own interpretation of Judaism. The Talmud Torah ostensibly was a community school, but its curriculum attracted primarily children of parents who belonged to the Conservative or Orthodox synagogues.

In 1968 the Reform synagogue operated a religious school with an enrollment of 466 students spread fairly evenly through all twelve public school grades. The Conservative synagogue also operated a large religious school with 482 students. The largest Orthodox synagogue (Sons of Jacob) ran a religious school with about 100 students. In addition, an Orthodox day school located in a northwestern suburb of Minneapolis, Torah Academy, had twelve children from St. Paul enrolled in 1968.

The great majority of children enrolled in synagogue schools (about 90 percent) received a Reform or Conservative religious training. It appeared that the continuity of Orthodox Judaism in St. Paul will be sustained only by a small minority, since only about 10 percent of the children who received a synagogue education in 1968 were enrolled in Orthodox schools.

In addition to education for children, the three largest synagogues operated programs for adult education. These programs were usually of a more informal nature than the religious schools for children. They included seminars, guest lecturers, and some more formal classes.

Center and Club

In the sphere of leisure activities two organizations predominated: the local Jewish community center and the Jewish country club. In 1968 the center served an estimated 4000 people, 10 to 12 percent of whom were non-Jews. It was estimated that this organization served about one-third the members of the St. Paul Jewish community. The center was located in the Highland Park area; when it was located in the Holly-Grotto area, it served only about 1500 people.[6]

The Hillcrest Country Club of St. Paul was organized in 1944 with about 100 members in response to the fact that Jews were not welcome at existing clubs. By 1968 the club had 250 members, which probably represented a total of about 1000 persons using its services, or 10 percent of the total population. (Some St. Paul Jews belonged to a Minneapolis country club.)

The club and center, of course, did not exhaust the range of possibilities of formal organizations that provided recreational activities. The synagogues with their auxiliary organizations and varied programs provided another context for leisure-time activities.

A listing of Jewish organizations in St. Paul for 1900, 1907, 1937, and 1966 indicated that the total number of organizations in St. Paul was 16, 31, 87, and 53, respectively. The rise and decline in the number of associations reflected the growth of the community and its organizational heterogeneity. By 1966 the community had decreased in size, and its organizations had to some extent consolidated.

Philanthropic and Welfare Organizations

The United Jewish Fund and Council was the central fund-raising agency for the Jewish community. According to its pledge card, in 1968 it served thirty-two national, local, state, and overseas agencies through the collection and disbursement of funds from among the Jews of St. Paul.

In 1968 it provided funds for eleven local welfare, educational, and social organizations. The United Jewish Fund and Council came closest to being a central Jewish organization, probably having contact with more Jews than any other organization in the city.

The Jewish Family Service of St. Paul provided family counsel to members of the community. In 1968 this counsel was largely in the area of parent-child relations. The goal of the Jewish Vocational Service was to help young people in career planning. In 1968 it was administering a Neighborhood Youth Corps project of the federal government as the only approved counseling service in St. Paul.

In addition to these agencies there were two centers for the elderly: the Sholom-Residence and the Jewish Home for the Aged of the Northwest.

Two regional agencies in the Twin Cities Metropolitan area also dealt with the relations between the Jewish community and the larger community: the Jewish Community Relations Council of Minnesota and the Anti-Defamation League of B'nai B'rith. A proliferation of other organizations, many involved in welfare and philanthropic work as well as educational, social, and cultural activities, also existed in St. Paul.

Jewish Esthetic and Intellectual Life

The organization of the esthetic and intellectual activities of the Jewish community occurred largely through the synagogues. They undertook independently to periodically set up art exhibits, musical concerts, and public lectures usually on Jewish themes or with famous Jewish personalities. In addition, the part of the service devoted to the sermon often functioned as a vehicle for presenting ideas from secular philosophy, politics, and literature as well as from traditional Jewish sources.

Summary

The history of the St. Paul Jewish community may be divided into four distinct phases. The period from around 1850 to 1880 saw the growth of the early community with the emergence of a cleavage between the East European and German Jews. The next period, from 1880 to 1930, witnessed a mass immigration of Jews from Eastern Europe, which led to the separation into two communities marked by differences in ritual observance, residence, language, social contacts, and socioeconomic status. The third phase, between 1930 and 1954 represented the period of transition into a unified community with movement toward organizational and social consolidation due to the pressures of anti-Semitism, the Depression, World War II, and the formation of the State of Israel. The fourth and contemporary period, beginning in 1954, has been highlighted by the building of synagogue and communal centers and the continued residential concentration in an upper-middle-class suburban area of St. Paul known as Highland Park. During the latter two periods the proportion of Jews decreased, primarily because of the decline in immigration and the increase of emigration from St. Paul.

Although St. Paul Jewry can be described as having three loosely defined social classes (the elite, less elite, and non-elite), these are internal distinctions. Over-all, the community's members belonged to the middle and upper strata of St. Paul. Key community decisions were made by the leadership of the larger community organizations. With respect to synagogue affiliation, the Conservative congregation predominated, followed by the Reform congregation, with the Orthodox group divided into a number of much smaller congregations. About one-quarter of the families in St. Paul did not belong to a synagogue. While Jewish education in this community continued to be marked by the primacy of Talmud Torah, its enrollment has been slowly declining in the past few years.

3   Methods and Measures

Writing in *The Jerusalem Post* about a study of Jewish identity in a midwestern suburb, the reviewer, Geoffrey Wigoder made the following observation:

Much is spoken and written about American Jewry (as well as other Jewries) on the basis of "hunches" without any tested foundation. To a large extent, this is inevitable owing to the absence of scientific investigation into the social phenomena motivating the community. However, in the U.S. (and more slowly, elsewhere) a series of studies in various areas are helping the formulation of more soundly-based conclusions regarding the present state of U.S. Jewry and the prognostication of future trends. There is still far to go and, so far, only few aspects have been systematically studied . . . but each new work fits another piece into the total jigsaw (1968: 11).

Our study, using contemporary conceptual and analytic sociological tools, furthers this work by empirically investigating Jewish group identification in an American community.

How the Research Was Done

The analysis to be presented in the succeeding sections is based on data originally gathered in the spring of 1969 in the Jewish community of St. Paul. (A complete discussion is found in the Methodological Appendix.) To ascertain some of the shifts in socialization processes and contemporary characteristics occurring in the community, data were collected from two generations of Jewish men, the majority of whom were father and son pairs. Even in this era of women's liberation it is still difficult to follow generations of mothers and daughters, because family names follow the male line; hence, the study was limited to men. The primary population from which data were gathered was a group of young men between the ages of twenty-two and twenty-nine inclusive who were living in metropolitan St. Paul. Ausubel (1954: 225) and Middleton and Putney (1963) have pointed out the advantages of detachment and greater objectivity in using young adults rather than adolescents to study socialization experiences retrospectively. (Since about four-fifths of Jews attend college immediately after high school, by age twenty-two most would have completed their undergraduate education.) Because the St. Paul community was not very large (10,500 in

33

1970) all persons in the age cohorts twenty-two through twenty-nine were included for study.

The older generation included fathers of the younger men living in the St. Paul area. The actual listing of the members of the two populations were constructed primarily through the examination of available lists of synagogues and other Jewish organizations. The cooperation of organization officials and publicizing of the project in the local press also aided this effort. While the two categories of respondents represented generations of fathers and sons, only the latter constituted a cohort (following Blau and Duncan, 1967: 81-83). Therefore, intergenerational analysis in terms of kinship (fathers and sons), age grade (older and younger), and to a lesser extent immigration (second and third) is possible. Intercohort analysis is not possible because the father's age at the time of his son's birth has a large variance.

Mail questionnaires were sent out to all individuals in the two generations. The questionnaires, each with a cover letter including a list of community sponsors, were mailed out during the first week of March 1969. During the following four weeks two reminders and another questionnaire were sent out. In sum, 302 usable questionnaires were returned, constituting 63 percent of the total possible cases. This total included 183 younger men (64 percent) and 119 of the older men (63 percent). Among these returns were 98 pairs of fathers and sons, which provided the opportunity to conduct the matched-pair analysis discussed in chapters 4 and 5.

Who the Respondents Were

Our investigation of Jewish identification is based on the data provided by the two generations of men in this community.[1] For a fuller appreciation of the issues and information with which we will deal and to make comparisons with other groups possible, we present some background information on the social characteristics of these respondents. We shall refer to the younger generation as sons and the older generation as fathers.

Approximately 90 percent (156) of the young men traced their paternal ancestry to Eastern Europe. Only a small number, however, claimed German ancestry. Ethnicity among the Jews of St. Paul—despite the community's history—was no longer a significant basis of social differentiation. About two-thirds (119) were third-generation Americans or grandsons of immigrants. The rest were evenly divided between second and fourth generations. A high proportion (69 percent) of these young men were born and raised in St. Paul. Ten percent moved to St. Paul when they were twenty-two or older.

Sixty-five percent of the young men in this study were married. Thirty-

Table 3-1
Occupational Levels by Generation
(Percent)

	Generation		
Occupational Level	Sons	Fathers	Grand-fathers
1. Higher Executives, Proprietors of Large Concerns, and Major Professionals	32	40	8
2. Business Managers, Proprietors of Medium-Sized Businesses, and Lesser Professionals	28	14	16
3. Administrative Personnel, Small Independent Businesses, and Minor Professionals	30	26	29
4. Clerical and Sales Workers, Technicians, and Owners of Little Businesses	7	13	20
5. Skilled Manual Employees	1	3	15
6. Machine Operators and Semiskilled Employees	1	3	7
7. Unskilled Employees	1	1	4
TOTAL	100	100	99 [b]
	(N=135) [a]	(N=118)	(N = 113)

Note: Occupations of grandfathers were ascertained on fathers' questionnaires.
[a]48 of sons were students.
[b]Error due to rounding.

one percent had preschool children, and 7 percent had school-age children. The data presented here should not be considered as indicative of marriage patterns or family size of Jewish families in general, since the respondents were all between twenty-two and twenty-nine. In this age range many young men are in the marriage market, and many of those who are already married can be expected to have more children.

Among the fathers, 94 percent traced their Old World nationality to East European countries. The great majority (76 percent) were second generation or the sons of immigrants. Eight percent were immigrants themselves, and the remainder were third- and fourth-generation Americans. While the coincidence is not perfect, fathers were for the most part second generation and sons third.

Most of the older men were longtime St. Paulites. Fifty-one percent were born in St. Paul, compared to 28 percent who were twenty-two or over when they moved to this community. Forty-seven percent of the older men had two children, 30 percent had three, and 22 percent had four or more children. Fifty-four percent of all fathers had children who were still in school.

Table 3-1 gives the proportion of men in each of seven occupational levels for sons, fathers and grandfathers.[2] The greatest shift occurred from the generation of grandfathers to fathers. While one-quarter of the former were in the upper two occupational levels, more than one-half of the fathers were in these two levels. In addition, there has been a steady decline from the grandfathers to the sons in the proportion in levels 4 and 5, which represent the traditional American middle-class occupations. It is important to note that 26 percent of the 183 younger respondents were students and not yet in the occupational hierarchy. Furthermore, many of the employed younger men are at the beginning of their careers and can be expected to move up in occupational rank.

The data on education for sons show that 20 percent had advanced degrees, 49 percent had college degrees, 25 percent had some college education, and only 7 percent had no college experience. Again it should be noted that forty-eight of these respondents were still matriculating. The older generation was also highly educated with 32 percent having college degrees, 29 percent having one to three years of college, 27 percent having completed high school, leaving only 13 percent who did not graduate from high school. The mean educational level for both fathers and sons was well above the national average.

The income distribution for sons excluding students was 34 percent, $12,000 or more; 52 percent, between $8000 and $12,000; and only 14 percent less than $8000. Since the age range was twenty-two to twenty-nine, it is very probable that their incomes will rise in the ensuing years in accord with their educational and occupational attainments.

While this distribution indicates a high level of income in comparison to the national average in 1969, it is overwhelmingly surpassed by the income distribution of the older generation: 25 percent, over $30,000; 25 percent, 16,000-$30,000; 21 percent, $12,000-$16,000; 19 percent, $8000-$12,000; and 9 percent, incomes of under $8000. With a total of 50 percent having incomes of $16,000 and more, the financial status of the older generation is rather affluent in comparison to both the total Jewish as well as American population. The income levels and occupations of the younger generation indicate that this characterization will continue to apply.

How Jewish Identification Was Measured

The measurement of facets of Jewish identity and identification has not been uniform. Rosen (1965) in his study of Jewish religiosity among York-town adolescents utilized four dimensions of group identification dealing with (1) ethnic group companionship, (2) ethnic group solidarity, (3) resistance to adopting outgroup practices, and (4) orientation toward opinions of ethnic comembers. The scores on the various items were added together and treated as one index.

In some cases Jewish "religiosity" itself is equated with group identification, as in the study of the Providence Jewish community conducted by Goldstein and Goldscheider (1968). They examined four dimensions of religiosity: (1) ideology, (2) ritual practice, (3) organizational involvement, and (4) cultural aspects. In a study of Protestants and Jews in Chicago, Lazerwitz (1970) found eight components of "religious group identification": (1) religious behavior (in terms of church or synagogue attendance), (2) pietism (or personal religious experience), (3) religious education, (4) religious organizational involvement, (5) traditional and current beliefs, (6) attitudes toward and concern for coreligionists, (7) the parental role (in terms of childhood and religious memories and in terms of actual or intended Jewish education of their children, and (8) friendship and courtship patterns. In both of these studies religiosity or religious group identification actually referred to the broader notion of ethnic group identification.

As a final example we may look at Sklare and Greenblum's study of Jewish identity in Lakeville (1967). The authors examined group identification in terms of ritual observance, synagogue attendance, concern for Israel, organizational involvement, friendship ties, and the image of the "good Jew."

While there is a core meaning for the concept of Jewish identification, there have been a variety of attempts to create scales and indices measuring this phenomenon. In some cases single questions aimed at tapping one dimension of Jewish identification have been used. On the other hand, multi-item scales directed at measuring Jewish identification in general have also been employed (Segalman, 1967). Such measurement has focused on attitudes, current behavior, intended behavior, or some combination of them. Given this variety, an operational definition of our conceptualization of Jewish identification is necessary.

JI Scale

In a recent essay Charles Liebman suggested that the ideology of American Jewry most closely paralleled the ideology of Reconstructionist Judaism (briefly described in chapter 2). Among the beliefs Liebman offers as shared by American Jewry in general and Reconstructionism are:

The Jews constitute one indivisible people. It is their common history and experience, not a common religious belief, that define them as a people. What makes one a Jew is identification with the Jewish people, and this is not quite the same as identification with the Jewish religion (1970:69).

Here we see the centrality of identification with Jewish peoplehood, in contrast to Jewish religion, a point supported by the Israeli Supreme Court decisions discussed in chapter 1. It would appear then that the key to studying Jewish identification lies in measuring the general attitudes toward Jewry rather than specific aspects of ritual practice, organizational involvement, pietism, etc.

Thirty-one items in our questionnaire measured various attitudes toward specific and general aspects of Jewish life. These items were subjected to a factor analysis. Factor analysis is a statistical technique that pulls out the most highly intercorrelated items into factors. (See Methodological Appendix for more details.) This analysis indicated that seven variables loaded highest on the first factor. These items constituted the Jewish Identification (JI) Scale. Each item was measured on a four-point Likert scale with responses ranging from strongly agree, agree, disagree, to strongly disagree. The items were:

1. I feel an attachment to the local Jewish community.
2. I feel an attachment to American Jewry.
3. Of all foreign countries, I feel the strongest ties to Israel.
4. I feel a strong attachment to Jewish life.
5. My general outlook has been affected by my sharing in the Jewish culture.
6. [I] think it is important to know the fundamentals of Judaism.
7. [I] feel a close kinship to the Jewish people throughout the world.

Much of the discussion that follows serves to demonstrate the validity of the JI Scale. These items loaded on other factors as well, indicating that Jewish identification is complicated by other, more particularistic dimensions. Nevertheless, these seven items define a general attitude toward the Jewish people and Jewish life. A few examples will illustrate the distinction. Among the items *not* included in the scale was: "[I] think it is important that Israel remain a Jewish State." Such an item indicates a more particularistic Zionist identification than does the statement (item 3): "Of all foreign countries I feel the strongest ties to Israel." Another example of this distinction between general and particularistic dimensions may be seen in comparing item 6, ([I] think it is important to know the fundamentals of Judaism") and the following item: "[I] feel the Torah is the revealed word of God." The latter item, not included in the scale, indicates a distinctively Orthodox point of view indicating a belief in divine revelation, whereas item 6, included in the scale, represents a belief in the importance of knowledge of Judaism, with which a secular Jew could agree. Further illustration of the more general nature of the scale is that the item with the highest loading (the item most highly intercorrelated with all the others) is the most direct measure of Jewish identification: "I feel a strong attachment to Jewish life."

Personal Profiles

In order to describe more clearly the nature of the JI Scale, we selected the five highest and lowest scorers and examined some of their social characteristics. Let us first describe the low-scorers. All names are fictitious.

Mr. Greene is twenty-five and married with no children. Having graduated from college he is working in sales. He has recently moved to St. Paul and is living adjacent to the downtown with no Jewish neighbors. A fourth-generation American, Mr. Greene did not receive a Jewish education and is not a member of a synagogue nor any other Jewish organization.

Mr. Baum is twenty-two and single. He has a college degree and is temporarily out of town working as a teacher in a federal government program. He moved to St. Paul as a youngster and makes his home with his parents in Highland Park, but at his temporary residence he has no Jewish neighbors. A third-generation American, Mr. Baum received no Jewish education and presently does not belong to a synagogue nor any other Jewish organization.

Mr. Land is twenty-four years old and married with no children. He is enrolled in a Ph.D. program in another state. A third-generation American, he moved to St. Paul as a youngster. He did not receive a Jewish education and presently does not belong to a synagogue nor any Jewish organization. Where Mr. Land is living now, he has no Jewish neighbors.

Dr. Gorson is twenty-eight and married with no children. He earned a Ph.D. and is now a college professor. Dr. Gorson is a fourth-generation American, born in St. Paul, who did not receive a Jewish education. He is not presently a member of a synagogue, nor of a Jewish organization. He is living in an area where there are no other Jews.

Mr. Meyerson in twenty-four and also married with no children. He attended college for two years and now works as a mechanical designer. He moved to St. Paul a few years ago and lives in a suburb with a few Jewish neighbors. Mr. Meyerson is a fourth-generation American who did not receive a Jewish education. Although he is not a member of a Jewish organization or synagogue, he does attend services occasionally.

These low-scorers have a number of common characteristics. They are all members of the younger generation, and while four are married, none has children. Four have at least an undergraduate college degree, and all work in a bureaucratic profession. Four were not born in St. Paul. At the time the data were collected, none was living within the area of Jewish residential concentration, Highland Park, and only one had any Jewish neighbors. The low-scorers did not receive a Jewish education, and they were not members of a synagogue or other Jewish organization. Thus, in terms of educational background, employment, and residence patterns they were not socially integrated into the Jewish community of St. Paul;

moreover, they had no basis for being integrated into the community subculture by virtue of their past religious education nor their present patterns of participation in voluntary associations.

At the other end of the scale, twenty-five persons were tied for the highest score. Of these, five were randomly selected for further examination.

Mr. Cohen is fifty years old and married with four children. He is a high-school graduate who is president of his own company and earning over $30,000. He is a third-generation American who moved to St. Paul as a young adult. He has been living in Highland Park for over twenty years, where half of his neighbors are Jewish. Mr. Cohen received a Jewish education beyond Bar Mitzvah. He is a member of the Conservative synagogue and attends services on the High Holidays and occasionally at other times. He has held a major office in two Jewish organizations.

Mr. Goldman is fifty-one and married with three children. He has some college experience and is a partner in a retail business earning over $30,000. A second generation American, he moved to St. Paul in his mid-twenties and has lived in Highland Park for over twenty years. Of Austrian descent, he belongs to the Reform synagogue and attends services on High Holidays and occasionally at other times. Mr. Goldman had only one or two years of Jewish education. He does not actively participate in any Jewish organizations.

Mr. Harris is forty-nine years old and is married with four children. He is a lawyer earning over $30,000. A second-generation American, he was born and raised in St. Paul and now lives in Highland Park. Mr. Harris received a post-Bar Mitzvah Jewish education. He is a member of the Conservative synagogue which he attends occasionally and is an active participant in three local Jewish organizations.

Mr. Silversmith is fifty-eight and married with two children. He is a college graduate, the president of his own firm, and earns between $16,000 and $30,000. He moved to St. Paul in his middle twenties and has lived in Highland Park for over twenty years. Mr. Silversmith is a second-generation American who received a Jewish education beyond his Bar Mitzvah. He is a member of the Conservative synagogue and attends synagogue occasionally during the year. He is a regular participant in three local Jewish organizations.

The fifth high-scorer is Mr. Silversmith's son. He is twenty-four and married with no children. He attended college but did not graduate. He is working in his father's business, earning over $12,000. He was born and raised in St. Paul and is now living in a suburb of Minneapolis with a high concentration of Jews. A third-generation Jew, he received a Jewish education that ended at about his Bar Mitzvah. He is not a member of any Jewish organizations except the Conservative synagogue he attends on the High Holidays.

The profiles of the high-scorers indicate several shared characteristics. Four are of the older generation and have at least two children. The high-scorers have varied educational experiences but are earning high incomes. The older-generation men have lived in Highland Park for a long time, where half of their neighbors are Jewish. The high-scorers received a Jewish education generally into the high-school level. They are synagogue members (usually Conservative) and attend services on the High Holidays and occasionally at other times. Three of the older men participate regularly in local Jewish organizations. The one high-scorer examined who was of the younger generation was not a college graduate. He worked for his father, who was also a high-scorer, suggesting the importance of the father's Jewish identification in affecting the son's. Thus, these high-scorers fit into the traditional pattern of Jewish community life. They were executives in private business firms or independent professionals who lived in the area of greatest Jewish concentration. They were integrated into the subcultural life of the community by their exposure to religious education and their activity and involvement in the synagogue or other Jewish organizations. In sum, those that scored very high or low on the JI Scale reflected their attitude in the pattern of their participation and involvement in Jewish community life in St. Paul.

JI and Related Measures

Thus far we have demonstrated that the JI Scale has "face validity," i.e., appears to get at the concept of Jewish identification on the face of it in terms of an examination of the items themselves and the high and low scorer profiles (Phillips, 1966: 159). Now we consider "construct validity," which is based on "the total set of propositions in which a concept is located" (Phillips, 1966: 161). In order to carry out this analysis, we examined the relationship of the JI Scale to several Jewish beliefs and attitudes thought to be related to Jewish identification.

Table 3-2 presents the correlation coefficients between the JI Scale and these several measures. The strongest association (.70) is between JI and Zionism, which was measured by a five-item index (see Methodological Appendix). This association may be understood in recalling that the data were collected less than two years after the Six Day War between Israel and the Arab states. Prior to the War, most Israeli and American Jews tended to view each other as distant relatives. The crisis created by the wartime situation prompted American Jewry to support Israel both in terms of volunteers and large sums of money, thereby establishing a closer relationship between two of the largest Jewish communities in the world. Thus, Israel represented for American Jews one of the most important symbols of group identification. Indeed, one of the items in the JI Scale, which was

Table 3-2
Zero-Order Correlation Coefficients (*r*) Between Jewish Identification (JI) Scale and Some Jewish Beliefs and Attitudes

Jewish Beliefs and Attitudes	Correlation with JI Scale
Zionism	.70
Ingroup Marriage	.57
Christmas Observance	.43
Orthodoxy	.40

$p < .001$ ($N = 298$).

constructed independently of the Zionism Index, reflected the role of Israel in Jewish identification: "Of all foreign countries, I feel the strongest ties to Israel."

The next strongest association (.57) was between JI and an item on ingroup marriage ("It is important to marry within the Jewish faith"), which was rated on a four-point Likert scale. This correlation probably represents two considerations: a concern with the maintenance of separation from the outgroup and a desire to perpetuate ties with other Jews. Given the concern in the Jewish community over intermarriage, one might have expected this item to be most highly correlated with the JI Scale. Intermarriage, however, tends to be greatest in large, growing Jewish communities and in very small areas (Lazerwitz, 1971: 42). Towns with small Jewish populations do not have sufficient numbers to organize themselves as a viable community and maintain a high rate of endogamy; cities with large concentrations of Jews provide many opportunities for individuals to move out of the network of community ties and possibly to marry outside the Jewish community. Since St. Paul fits between these two categories, we would expect that comparatively lower rates of intermarriage in this community would make the issue less salient here.

The correlation between the two-item Christmas Observance Index (see Methodological Appendix) and the JI Scale ($r = .43$) is significant but not as strong as either of those involving the preceding two measures. The more highly identified Jew probably does have stronger negative reactions toward celebrating Christmas, but Christmas comes once a year, and there are many ways of dealing with the strain it creates (see Gerson, 1965). Hence, it is a less salient factor than Zionism or intermarriage for Jews.

Finally, the lowest significant correlation ($r = .40$) is between the two item Orthodoxy Index (see Methodological Appendix) and JI. While such a belief is not central to Jewish identification in the United States (only a handful of the respondents in this study belonged to an Orthodox synagogue), it is, nevertheless, a salient factor for some Jews. Comparing the association of Zionism and Orthodoxy with the JI Scale, we see further support for Liebman's conclusion that the ideology of American Jewry reflects the primacy of peoplehood over religion (1970).

How the Generations Differ

During the past decade the popular press has printed countless feature articles on the generation gap. Analyses of generational conflict and differences, however, go back to the philosophers of antiquity. For contemporary sociologists, Karl Mannheim's work has been a key starting point in their studies of generations, particularly in relation to beliefs and attitudes. Mannheim argues that the succession of generations makes for a selective remembering and forgetting of the cultural heritage (1952: 292-302). Members of one generation have a "similarity of location," to use his term. They, therefore, experience the same events and do it with similar consciousness. This similarity comes primarily from sharing the same experiences as first impressions during childhood. These experiences form the generation's "natural view of the world" from which all other strata of experience are interpreted (1952: 298). Since any two successive generations, even of the same culture or subculture, must have differing perspectives, they always perceive different threats and problems.

For world Jewry major and indeed cataclysmic events have occurred during the last fifty years. Some of these events have affected American Jews less directly than their European brethren, but they have, nevertheless, been important aspects of the experiences of the two generations represented by the St. Paul Jewish men in this study. The same event affects American Jews in quite different ways depending on whether it enters into the natural view of the world (during childhood) or into adult consciousness. The immigrant community immersed in the East European Jewish culture was the place of the older respondents' formative years; the younger men know of such a community only through the nostalgic stories of their fathers or their grandfathers. The Nazi holocaust, both as a macabre, surrealistic, yet impossibly true representation of Jewish existence and as a personal tragedy for millions of living Jews, struck the older generation just as they were reaching their maturity; their sons were barely out of short pants. Today the terror of naziism still burns as a personal tragedy for many of the fathers; for most of the sons it appears as an historical, albeit a tragic, event. The founding of Israel, from the press reports of the blowing up of the King David Hotel in Jerusalem, to the radio broadcast of the U.N. vote on Israeli statehood, from the press coverage of the first Arab-Israeli war, to the reports of a miracle of nation-making during the first crucial years of independence, was part of the older generation's personal experience. The sons, however, had to wait for Leon Uris's *Exodus* (1958); most waited for the movie.

American anti-Semitism has probably affected, to a greater or lesser degree, all the respondents in this study, with or without their knowledge. The crucial difference is that when the older generation was in their twenties anti-Semitism was respectable. It wae practiced in vehement forms by some of the nation's culture heroes, such as Henry Ford and Father Coughlin. In the period of the younger generation's twenties, overt anti-Semitism was no longer generally accepted. These and other events have made the two age groups of men in this study into two historical Jewish generations.

Given the above considerations one would expect differences between the generations regarding aspects of Jewish identification. Indeed, much has been written on this topic; however, there is more than a little ambiguity on the nature of these generational changes. Probably the most popular view is represented in the following statement by Sherman:

Not only is the generation with the will and the interest to preserve ethnic identity in the U.S. [the immigrant generation] dying out; the generations that follow lack that interest and will. And the results are inevitable: all the evidence indicates that assimilation will proceed at a faster rate in the future than in the past (1961: 52).

On the other hand, Goldstein and Goldscheider write: "Second- and third-generation Jews did not lose their Jewish identity, and, perhaps, the sense of Jewish identification among third-generation Jews has increased" (1968: 9). How then do the two groups of respondents in this study compare on our Jewish Identification Scale and on our measures of related Jewish beliefs and attitudes? It is necessary to deal with this question before considering the possible sources and concomitants of Jewish identification. The answer to this question will help determine whether or not further analysis of Jewish identification should proceed along generational lines.

In this study the mean score on the Jewish Identification Scale for the fathers generation was significantly higher than that of the sons. Table 3-3 shows the JI Scale trichotomized into high, middle, and low scores for fathers and sons. While a little more than a third of each generation had middle-range scores, the more extreme scores vary significantly. Among the fathers, 42 percent had high scores compared to 28 percent of the sons. At the other extreme, 38 percent of sons had low scores, compared to 20 percent of the fathers. We have already discussed the historical experiences of these two generations that help explain these differences. Focusing on generational change in the St. Paul Jewish community, we might add that the West Side immigrant community in which most of the fathers grew up was a highly integrated, traditional Jewish community, while the areas

Table 3-3
Jewish Identification by Generation
(Percent)

Jewish Identification Scale	Generation	
	Fathers	Sons
Low	20	38
Middle	38	34
High	42	28
TOTAL	100	100
	(N = 119)	(N = 179)

$X^2 = 11.9$, $df = 2$, $p < .01$, gamma = .32.

Table 3-4
Orthodoxy by Generation
(Percent)

Orthodoxy	Generation	
	Fathers	Sons
Low	18	49
Middle	53	44
High	29	7
TOTAL	100	100
	(N = 119)	(N = 179)

$X^2 = 39.5$, $df = 2$, $p < .001$, gamma = .59.

of later Jewish settlement, including the present area, Highland Park, have a much more mixed pattern of Jewish and Gentile residence. Furthermore, most of the members of the older generation were in traditionally Jewish occupations like independent professions, trade, or skilled crafts, where they dealt in large part with other Jews. In contrast, the younger generation respondents were much more likely to be in occupations that brought them in contact only with members of the community at large.

Table 3-4 presents the differences in the levels of commitment to Orthodoxy for fathers and sons. Members of the older generation were more likely to score high (29 percent) on our Index of Orthodoxy than were the younger respondents (7 percent). On the other hand, approximately half of the sons scored low in comparison to less than one-fifth the fathers. This is not surprising, since only a few younger men in St. Paul belonged to an Orthodox synagogue. This pattern of membership is not unlike other communities. For example, Goldstein and Goldscheider found that in Provi-

Table 3-5
Zionism by Generation
(Percent)

	Generation	
Zionism	Fathers	Sons
Low	19	43
Middle	38	28
High	43	28
TOTAL	100	99[a]
	(N = 119)	(N = 180)

$X^2 = 18.7$, $df = 2$, $p < .001$, gamma $= .37$.
[a]Error due to rounding.

dence only a small percent of the younger persons (aged twenty-five to forty-four) of the third generation were members of an Orthodox synagogue (1968: 177). Axelrod, Fowler, and Gurin reported a similar finding in Boston (1967: 122). Nevertheless, synagogue membership and ideology need not be congruent.

The process of secularization has been operating to weaken the Orthodox belief system that dominated Jewish religious life in Eastern Europe. As Sklare has observed:

a substantial segment of those who arrived in the United States during the great wave of East European immigration were at best nominally Orthodox. They had already felt the impact of secularization before they left Europe and the process gained considerable momentum in the United States. Thus the experience of many native-born Jews—even those who are members of the second or third generation—has been to grow up in a household where the hold of secular values was strong.

We may conclude that successive generations as represented in our study show a general trend away from traditional religious belief.

There were also differences in the strength of Zionism between fathers and sons (see table 3-5). Fathers were more likely than sons to score higher on our Index of Zionism. This finding reflects the greater assimilation of the younger generation, who are more likely to unequivocally view America as the homeland rather than Israel. Perhaps the difference between the generations would have been greater but for the fact that the Six Day War had occurred less than two years earlier. The crisis of the spring of 1967 had a great impact on all generations of American Jewry, generating both an outpouring of finanacial contributions and young volunteers.

In comparing Orthodoxy and Zionism we see that the generational differences are stronger for the former (gamma = .59) than the latter (gamma = .37). While secularization has weakened the traditional cove-

Table 3-6
Ingroup Marriage Belief by Generation
(Percent)

	Generation	
Ingroup Marriage Belief	*Fathers*	*Sons*
Disagree	5	28
Agree	43	42
Strongly Agree	52	30
TOTAL	100	100
	(N=119)	(N=181)

$X^2 = 28.3$, $df = 2$, $p < .001$, gamma = .49.

nant relationship between the Jewish people and God, a sense of Jewish nationalism has strengthened the bonds of the Jewish people toward their traditional homeland. Judaism has traditionally been based on the unity of the people, the religion, and the land of Israel. Our findings reported in the previous section, that Jewish identification was more strongly related to Zionism than Orthodoxy and the fact that the generations are more sharply divided over Orthodoxy than Zionism suggest that the sense of Jewish peoplehood and nationhood is stronger than the commitment to traditional Jewish religion.

Difference in intermarriage rates between the generations are often taken as evidence for the diminution of Jewish identification in the third generation compared to the second. While this is probably partially true, two points should be kept in mind. First, the overwhelming majority (about 80 percent) of marriages in the third generation are still endogamous. Second, all intermarriages cannot be interpreted as a denial of Jewish identification; in some the non-Jewish partner converts to Judaism. As Sklare puts it, "The Jew who intermarries, then, generally does so because he wishes to *marry* rather than because he wishes to intermarry" (1971: 201). Nevertheless, there do appear to be major differences in the belief about the desirability of ingroup marriage between the two generations of Jewish men in this study (see table 3-6). In responding to the statement "It is important to marry within the Jewish faith," more than 50 percent of the fathers strongly agreed compared to 30 percent of the respondents in the younger generation. At the other extreme almost 30 percent of the sons disagreed with this statement compared to 5 percent of the older-generation men.[3]

In a classroom discussion dealing with the question of the two main barriers to intermarriage among Jews, one of our students immediately offered: "Mother and Father." This is certainly part of the answer, but from a sociological perspective the barriers are the concern with the covenant of faith and the solidarity of the people, including one's family ties. Since it has already been noted that the younger generation deemphasizes the traditional religious aspect of Jewish identification, we would argue that the difference in the belief about ingroup marriage is more a function of changes in this area than in identification with the Jewish people and with one's family. Most of those in the younger generation, however, favor endogamous marriage even when the issue is phrased as generally as it is here.

Summary

In this chapter we discuss how the research was done; how Jewish identification was measured; the relationship between the JI Scale and specific Jewish beliefs and attitudes; and differences between the generations regarding Jewish identification and these other beliefs and attitudes.

Our data were provided by questionnaires filled out by 183 Jewish men residing in St. Paul, aged twenty-two to twenty-nine, inclusive, and 119 men who were fathers of those in the younger population. While we have "fathers" without "sons" and vice versa, there were ninety-eight father-son pairs among the respondents. The questionnaire contained questions on a wide range of social background characteristics as well as items used to indicate a number of particular issues including Jewish identification and other Jewish-related attitudes and practices.

Concerning general social characteristics, almost all the respondents, both younger and older, are middle or upper-middle class. Further, the entire group is characterized by exceptionally high educational and occupational attainment. The incomes for the older generation are also very high, and it is projected that the younger men will follow suit. Turning to the key factors discussed in this chapter, Jewish identification was measured by a seven-item scale. These items were selected using a factor analysis of thirty-one items that appeared in the questionnaire. The item with the highest factor loading was "I feel a strong attachment to Jewish life." This chapter also contains five profiles of high JI Scale scorers and five profiles of the low scorers. The profiles and the content of the scale items themselves indicate the "face validity" of the JI Scale. The "construct validity" of the scale is assessed by its association with certain attitudes and beliefs related to Jewish identification. Specifically, JI was correlated with a Zionism Index ($r = .70$); with an Ingroup marriage item ($r = .57$); with a Christmas Observation Index ($r = .43$); and with Orthodoxy ($r = .40$). Reasons for each of these associations and for the differences between the correlations are discussed.

The last part of this chapter is devoted to a consideration of differences between the generations on Jewish identification and the Jewish beliefs and attitudes presented above. The notion of generation includes more than merely attributes such as age, parent-child distinction, or relationship to migration. Generation also refers to the location of individuals in a particular social, cultural, and historical milieu that shapes their experience. For instance, college life, the Vietnam War, "living together," and the drug scene represent a part of this aspect of generational experience.

For both theoretical and empirical reasons, being Jewish may best be assessed in terms of the generational factor. In this regard fathers were higher on the JI Scale, on Orthodoxy, on Zionism, and on Ingroup marriage. Based on the data and analysis in this chapter, the sources and concomitants of Jewish identification are treated separately according to generation in the following chapters.

4

Becoming A Jew: The Younger Generation

According to the intergroup relations explanation of minority group identification, if outgroup hostility remains at a particular level, then minority
group identification should also remain at a given level. Let us for a moment
consider this in reference to the black American experience over the last
ten years. While economic, political, and social conditions have improved,
at least for some, black people are undoubtedly still an oppressed minority.
Furthermore, their position in this country's social structure has changed
but little. In spite of this, however, there has been a marked change in black
group identification and self-concept. Black people are becoming more and
more involved with a sense of group identification and a concomitant
positive black identity (see National Advisory Commission on Civil Disorders, 1968; Pinkney, 1969). This change, we would argue, is due in large
part to changing patterns of interpersonal relations within the black community. Black people, particularly younger ones, are creating and involving themselves with groups that provide a positive frame of reference,
such as various black student groups and community organizations and, on
a more limited basis, organizations like the Black Panthers and the Black
Muslims. Furthermore, both within and outside of these groups, blacks are
developing interpersonal relations with one another which promote a sense
of group identification. While much has been written on these phenomena,
particularly on black organizations (Lincoln 1961, Essien-Udom, 1962),
there has been little empirical research on how these reference groups and
interpersonal relations affect identification.

While our study of an advantaged (at least, economically) ethnic minority does not deal directly with the black American experience, the processes by which American Jews have maintained their Jewish identification
through attachments to reference groups and significant others is finding
increasing parallels in the American black community. It is our contention
that the experiences recounted by the respondents in this research are part
and parcel of the positive, interpersonal creation and affirmation of group
identification for whatever the group in question: blacks, Chicanos, Indians, Puerto Ricans, Mormons, Children of God, Flat-Earthers, or, as in
this case, Jews.

Our approach considers the interpersonal level of ethnic identification.
On this level other persons directly affect the individual, influencing him by
their own behavior and attitudes. Furthermore, they also indirectly affect

his identification by mediating and supporting the individual's attachment to the group's organizations and institutions. Many experiences enter into ethnic identification. Often it is difficult, indeed impossible, to say that a particular phenomenon is a causal factor. More often than not, the factors are interdependent. For instance, is membership in a particular ethnic organization a cause or a result of ethnic identification? While recognizing this issue, our approach in this chapter is to concentrate on factors that we believe are likely to contribute to Jewish identification, and to do this for one crucial phase of the life cycle.

Ethnic identification begins in childhood. Some research (Clark and Clark, 1958; Hartley, 1948) indicates that even before a child reaches his teens, the process is already well underway. The period of adolescence is often considered crucial in the formation and stabilization of ethnic identification (Rosen, 1965). However, just as this process does not end in childhood, it does not end in adolescence. Ethnic identification is enhanced or attenuated by adult experiences as well. While recognizing the potentially lifelong process involved in developing, maintaining, or changing one's Jewish identification, we agree with those who view adolescence as a key period and, hence, focus our research on this stage.

As sociologists, we are inclined to look first at the individual's relationships with others in studying his Jewish identification. However, each person is involved in a number of relationships even if we limit our analysis to adolescence. The relationships that are most salient for the individual are those with *significant others*, persons with whom an individual interacts who have an important influence on his thinking and behavior (Stryker, 1964: 139). According to Rosen, "the individual's attitudes either directly reflect those held by significant others, or are formed within a frame of reference created by significant others" (1965: 66).

We are concerned, however, with the effect of collectivities of individuals as well as of significant others. Such collectivities can be networks of interacting individuals (a social group) or a number of people having the same position or attribute (a social category). When people as collectivities create a frame of reference in which the individual develops his ethnic identification (among other attitudes) we employ the term *reference group* (Shibutani, 1955: 44).

Thus, we seek to determine the relative influence of various significant others and reference groups, which taken together represent the agents of socialization to ethnic identification. What follows, then, is an empirical examination of the interpersonal influences in becoming a Jew.

The Family

It is a sociological axiom that the family is the basic agent of socialization.

Based largely on Cooley's seminal analysis of "primary group" influence (1909) and Freud's theory of personality development (1938), sociologists have specified and elaborated upon this axiom (Stryker, 1964). However, some sociologists note a lessening influence of the family upon its members. While recognizing that the family "has been the prime mechanism for transmitting Jewish identity," Sklare argues further: "This system of identity-formation is currently on the decline. The emerging crisis of the Jewish family in identity-formation is in part due to the newer limitations on the family as a socialization agent—limitations that affect all other Americans as well" (1971: 99). Even if one grants this, it appears to us that the family is still the most important factor in Jewish identification. Furthermore, we contend that the family is not only the chief "mechanism" by which this attitude is transmitted, but the most important *source* of Jewish identification as well. In other words, the content of family life, the attitudes and practices of family members, contain many of the transmitted elements of Jewish identification. This appears to be what Sebald means when he writes, "Jewish family life is interwoven with ethnic practices, thus giving the children the immense psychological benefit of a number of meaningful rituals and ceremonies that mark religious observances, holidays, family events, and rites of passage"(1968: 290).

One additional issue in considering the importance of family is the fact that we are focusing on socialization during the adolescent period. There is much popular discussion of the disparity between adolescent and adult attitudes and values and of the lack of parental influence on their adolescent children. However, these discussions, often subsumed under the title "generation gap," have not been supported by empirical research (see Campbell, 1969). For instance, in a study of Jewish teenagers, Rosen found that about 90 percent stated that their parents' opinion was very important to them (1965). Regarding his respondents' religious traditionalism, Rosen stated, "There is a clear association between what parents expect and how the child thinks and behaves: the more traditionalistic the expectation level, the more likely it is that the adolescent will be traditionalistic in attitude and conduct" (1965: 74). In general, then, we contend that family influences, while possibly attenuated by restricted family responsibilities and nonfamily influences, particularly in adolescence, will be primary determinants of Jewish identification.

Starting with Mead (1934) the notion of the attitudes and expectations of others as a central element in the formation of an indiviudal's attitudes has been central to sociological social psychology. The literature on roles emphasizes the effect of expectations on the individual's behavior (see Biddle and Thomas, 1966). As Stryker notes, the expectations of significant others "are the most important for an individual's attitudes" (1964). In light of this analysis, we assessed the degree to which family members perceived by our respondents as significant others expected them to participate in

Table 4-1

Zero-Order Correlation Coefficients (r) Between JI Scale and Possible Socialization Determinants (Sons)

Possible Socialization Determinants	Correlation with JI Scale
Family	
Index of Jewish Expectations (IJE)	.30
Index of Jewish Activities (IJA: with parents)	.24
Older Brother (Presence)	.23
Father	
Religiosity	.33
JI Scale Score	.29[a]
Peers	
Index of Jewish Expectations (IJE)	.29
Index of Jewish Activities (IJA)	.15
Jewish Education	.23

Note: All correlation coefficients were significant at $p < .05$ with $N = 173$.
[a] $< .01$, $N = 98$.

Jewish activities during adolescence. Our measure, an Index of Jewish Expectations (IJE), consisted of the summated scores of the degree of perceived expectation for participation (rated very weak, weak, strong, very strong) from significant others. These scores were weighted according to whether the significant other was listed as the first, second, or third most important person to the respondent during his adolescence. (See the Methodological Appendix for a detailed discussion of the index.) It is our contention that the expectations from family members measured in this index would be a significant factor in determining the strength of Jewish identification. In fact, the correlation (r) between the Index of Jewish Expectations from family members and the Jewish Identification Scale was statistically significant at .30 (see table 4-1).

The Index of Jewish Expectations indicates something of the extent to which the family's, and particularly the parent's (77 percent of family significant others were parents), attitudes are important for Jewish identification. It does not tell us, however, the extent to which our respondents actually engaged in Jewish-related activities with their parents. We believe that such behavior would also be an important factor in Jewish identification. A number of leading attitude theorists have argued and provided evidence for viewing behavior as a determinant of attitudes in contrast to the more common opposite view (Festinger, 1957; Bem, 1970). They see attitudes as forming to coincide and be consistent with the actual behavior of the individual. For our purposes this behavior is Jewish activities undertaken with one's parents during adolescence. To measure this factor, an Index of Jewish Activities (IJA) was constructed. This index was based on a list of Jewish activities that might take place during adolescence. Our respondents checked those activities in which they participated and indicated with whom (parents, friends, or others) they took place. Examples of listed activities are "discussed topics with Jewish themes," "spoke Yiddish," and "attended a Jewish camp." (See the Methodological Appendix for a fuller discussion of this index.) It is our contention that this behavioral aspect of our respondents' adolescent family Jewish experiences would be a factor in the shaping of Jewish identification. We found that our measure of this experience, derived from the Index of Jewish Activities, was significantly correlated with the Jewish Identification Scale ($r = .24$, see table 4-1).

Our focus on familial determinants of Jewish identification has been on the effect of parents' attitudes and behavior. This emphasis on parental influence is consistent with sociological theory and research. However, the concept of significant other can be extended to include other family members. The most likely other relative to affect the adolescent male's Jewish identification would be his older brother. This person might provide a role-model similar to that of the father, thus possibly providing those attitudes and behaviors determinant of Jewish identification. Furthermore, by serving as a link to Jewish organizations and individuals, an older brother might contribute to the respondents' integration into the Jewish community, thereby fostering his sense of Jewish identification. Our findings indicate that the presence or absence of an older brother was significantly associated with the Jewish Identification Scale ($r = .23$, see table 4-1).

The Father

We have argued that having an older brother makes a difference for Jewish identification. If such is the case, what can be said for the influence of one's father? Jewish cultural patterns and the process of adolescent identification with the same-sex parent lead us to contend that the father would be the significant other with the greatest effect on our respondents' Jewish identification. While the popular literature dwells on the emotional and sexual problems caused the Jewish son by his castrating mother (Roth, 1967), the fact remains that Jewish religious, intellectual, and communal life in American society remains, as Jewish life has been throughout history, male dominated. The mother may decide what to make for the *Yontif* (holiday) meal; the father decides if and how *Yontif* will be celebrated. Furthermore, it is indeed the father who is cited most often as the single most important person in our respondents' adolescent experience. As a matter of fact, more than twice as many sons (32 percent) name their father as name their mother (15 percent). Finally, there is some evidence that while teen-age boys may feel closer to their mothers, emotionally they perceive themselves to be more like their fathers (Offer, 1969: 252).

In summary, it is our belief that relevant characteristics of the father will be among the most powerful determinants of Jewish identification. The two characteristics we have chosen to study assess central behavioral and attitudinal characteristics of our respondents' fathers which are most likely to be such determinants. Behaviorally, we use a measure of father's religiosity, constructed by multiplying the traditionalism score of synagogue affiliation (1. nonmember, 2. Reform, 3. Conservative, 4. Orthodox) and frequency of synagogue attendance score (1. never, 2. High Holidays only, 3. occasionally, 4. weekly, 5. daily). We argue that the extent of this behavioral measure of father's Jewish involvement, father's religiosity, will be a significant determinant of Jewish identification as measured by our scale. The correlation (r) between these two factors was statistically significant at .33 (table 4-1). Our attitudinal measure of a relevant characteristic of the fathers is their own Jewish Identification Scale scores. We have these scores for each of the ninety-eight fathers who can be paired with their sons' scores. It is our contention that the fathers' Jewish identification will be an important determinant of the same attitude on the part of their sons. The correlation (r) between the Jewish Identification Scale scores of fathers and sons was statistically significant at .29 (table 4-1).

Peers

While parents were selected as significant others 42 percent of the time, by far the most frequent choice, no more than about one-fifth of the respondents chose friends as among the three most important persons who influenced their thinking. Despite the pre-eminence of parents over peers in influencing our respondents' thinking, we would, nevertheless, anticipate a relationship between the extent of Jewish involvement with peers and Jewish identification.

Rosen, in his study of adolescent Jewish religiosity, summarized the sociological thinking on peer groups influence.

Whatever future research may reveal about the importance of the peer group in childhood and adulthood, it will probably suggest that at no other time in life is the peer group as important to the individual as in adolescence. In our society the lag between physiological and social maturity creates a host of problems for the adolescent. In his efforts to cope with these problems he often turns to his peers for companionship, recognition and support. The peer group provides the adolescent with a sense of belonging at a time when conflicting loyalties, identifications, and values make him unsure of himself (1965: 103-104).

Given the importance of peer group influence during adolescence, we would expect Jewish identification to be partly determined by the extent of Jewish involvement with peers. The processes by which significant others and reference groups affect the individual's attitudes and behavior can be applied to peer as well as family influence. As in the case of parents, we study the effect of peers in terms of expectations and activities, which we presume to be determinants of Jewish identification.

The Index of Jewish Expectations, discussed earlier, provided us with a measure of peer expectations from significant others for participation in Jewish activities. Peer expectations measured in this way were significantly associated with the JI Scale ($r = .29$, table 4-1). The behavioral aspect of peer influence utilized was the Index of Jewish Activities (see previous section). Our measure of participation in Jewish activities with peers was correlated with the JI Scale at the $r = .15$ level (table 4-1).

Jewish Education

Ackerman, in his summary of the literature on the relationship between Jewish education and Jewish identification among adolescents, suggests that the existing studies taken as a whole present an ambiguous picture of the effect of Jewish education on Jewish identification (1969: 23-24). It is our view, however, that the Jewish school is an important agent in socialization to Jewish identification both in terms of cognitive developemnt and interpersonal relationships. The curriculum provides the intellectual content (the knowledge of ideas, rituals, practices, etc.) which promotes and provides a basis for Jewish identification. Just as important is the interpersonal association with other Jews, both students and teachers, in the Jewish school. Such interpersonal relationships facilitate Jewish identification by developing group solidarity and by fostering attitudes and behavior appropriate for participation in the Jewish community. In sum, we believe that a number of influences are encompassed within Jewish education that in part determine the strength of Jewish identification.

The level of Jewish education was measured following Rosen (1965: 122) by multiplying the number of years by the number of hours per week that the respondent attended religious school. Thus, the product represented the number of "units" of Jewish education an individual received. The potential role of Jewish education as an agent in shaping Jewish identification is confirmed by our finding of a significant correlation between Jewish Education and the JI Scale ($r = .23$, table 4-1).

We have discussed the socialization factors (for which we have data available) that sociological theory would lead us to posit as possible determinants of ethnic identification. The statistical analysis of the independent effects of these variables is presented in Chapter 5. We are, of course, aware that there are other socialization factors that we have not systematically investigated. Information on mother's influence, the extended kin

58

network, and other specifications of significant other and reference group effects merit attention. So does assessment of communal and organizational effects during the adolescent years. However, our focus on immediate family (concentrating on father's influence), close friends, and Jewish school as socialization variables is consistent with our views of the crucial interpersonal determinants of ethnic identification among Jewish men.

Summary

In this chapter we briefly outline the theoretical basis for our study of some central determinants of Jewish identification and present the simple bivariate associations that relate to our propositions. We focus on adolescence as the key period in the formation of Jewish identification. During that period the teenager is involved in a number of relationships. Of greatest importance are relationships with individuals who have a more or less lasting effect on his thinking and behavior, *significant others*; and relationships with collectivities of people who create one's frame of reference, *reference groups*.

Family members constitute the primary significant others and reference group for most Jewish adolescents. The family provides both the mechanism and the content for Jewish identification. This is true in spite of much popular reference to the "generation gap." Our theoretical position led us to consider the family's expectations that their son participate in Jewish activities (measured by our Index of Jewish Expectations) and the actual Jewish activities that the adolescent engaged in with his parents (measured by our Index of Jewish Activities) as determinants of Jewish identification. Both family expectations and activities with parents were significantly related to the JI Scale. Focusing on individual family members as significant others, we found that those respondents having an older brother had significantly higher JI Scale scores than those who did not. The most important individual in the family was, however, as we would expect, the father. In particular, the father's religiosity and the father's own JI Scale score were related to the respondent's JI Scale score.

Considering the adolescent's other important reference group, his peers, both friends' expectations and activities with friends were correlated significantly with the JI Scale. Finally, we discuss our third area of socialization to Jewish identification: Jewish education. The Jewish school is here seen as instrumental both because of the intellectual content it provides and the interpersonal associations (fellow Jewish students and Jewish teachers) that occur within it. In effect, we contend that a number of influences toward Jewish identification are contained within Jewish education. Our data tend to confirm this contention, showing a significant correlation between Jewish education and Jewish identification.

In sum, we posit family, peers, and Jewish education as key determinants in Jewish identification. Our initial look at the relevant data, in terms of zero-order correlations, indicates that this is a productive course.

5

Adolescent Experience and Adult Activity

Several years ago a Jewish communal worker, associated with the YM-YWHAS of New York City, addressed an international conference of Jewish communal service workers in Jerusalem.

As practitioners we are concerned with the development of identity formation and its expression in the form of religio-ethnic identification as part of a *lifelong* process. Jewish identification—like life itself—is not a static condition, but rather a fluid quality, which we in the Jewish community center believe can be molded and strengthened. But we are likely to influence identification more if we seek to understand the components of identity formation (Brodsky, 1968: 258).

It is to this issue that we address ourselves in this chapter; to examine the effects not only of adolescent experience but also of adult activity in becoming a Jew for the younger generation of respondents.

Socialization Effects

We have discussed the socialization factors that we believed would be likely determinants of Jewish identification and which, indeed, were significantly correlated with the JI Scale. Our analysis so far has been confined to the degree of association between each socialization variable and the dependent variable, the JI Scale. This procedure, however, does not allow us to examine the combined effect of all of these variables that make a significant contribution to the explanation of Jewish Identification. The multiple correlation coefficient (R) represents this effect. We are interested in the multiple correlation coefficient in that "our primary interest . . . [is] in the explanatory power of a number of independent variables taken together, rather than in the relationship between the dependent variable and each of the independent variables taken separately" (Blalock, 1960: 346).

The R of .53 in table 5-1 indicates that roughly 28 percent (i.e., the square of .53) of the variance in the JI Scale is explained by these socialization variables taken together. Nevertheless, we still need a way of determining the relative contribution of each variable to the explanation of Jewish identification.

To do this we used regression analysis, which produces beta coeffi-

Table 5-1
Stepwise Multiple Regression Analysis: Socialization Determinants of Jewish Identification (Sons)

Step	Independent Variable	Beta Weight	F Ratio	Multiple R	R^2	R^2 Change
1	Father's Religiosity	.33	21.1	.33	.11	.11
2	Father's Religiosity	.29	17.4	.41	.17	.06
	Friends' Expectations (IJE)	.25	12.7			
3	Father's Religiosity	.28	15.7	.46	.21	.04
	Friends' Expectations (IJE)	.25	13.0			
	Jewish Education	.20	8.2			
4	Father's Religiosity	.24	11.6	.49	.24	.03
	Friends' Expectations (IJE)	.25	13.1			
	Jewish Education	.19	8.1			
	Activities with Parents (IJA)	.17	6.1			
5	Father's Religiosity	.22	10.3	.51	.26	.02
	Friends' Expectations (IJE)	.25	13.3			
	Jewish Education	.16	5.7			
	Activities with Parents (IJA)	.17	6.2			
	Older Brother	.16	5.2			
6	Father's Religiosity	.19	7.1	.53	.28	.02
	Friends' Expectations (IJE)	.23	11.6			
	Jewish Education	.15	5.0			
	Activities with Parents (IJA)	.14	4.3			
	Older Brother	.16	5.3			
	Family Expectations (IJE)	.13	3.5			

Note: All F Ratios significant with $DF = 1$, 171 in Step 1 to $DF = 6$, 166 in Step 6.

cients that may be compared to assess the relative contribution of each independent variable in accounting for the variance in the dependent variable (Graves and Lave, 1972). Thus, in examining table 5-1, the higher the beta value for a particular variable, the greater the contribution of that socialization factor to the determination of Jewish identification. Beta weights are standardized values of b, i.e., beta weights "indicate how much change in the dependent variable is associated with each unit of change in the dependent variable when the other variables are "controlled" (Graves and Lave, 1972:54). The value of the beta weight for one variable is to be interpreted by comparing it to the beta weights of other variables in the explanation.

Table 5-1 also presents the rest of the information from our regression analysis of socialization factors in Jewish identification, including the F ratio, which is a test of statistical significance; the Multiple R, which is the correlation coefficient of the independent variables and the dependent variable; the R^2, which when translated into percent gives the proportion of variance explained out of a maximum of 100 percent; and R^2 Change, which refers to the proportion of variance additionally explained by adding in another independent variable. This analysis utilizes the stepwise regression procedure, which enters each variable of a specified list according to its relative contribution to the total variance explained at that step. In the final step all the significant variables are recorded with their specific contribution to the explanation of the dependent variable in a form that is analogous to an equation.[1]

Father's Religiosity (Step 1)

The single most powerful socialization factor, according to the zero-order correlations, is father's religiosity. (As the first variable entered, the beta weight of .33 is equivalent to the zero-order correlation coefficient.) As noted in our discussion of the father's influence, he has the greatest effect on the adolescent male's Jewish identification. Furthermore, this particular variable, father's religiosity, measures a manifestly observable behavioral characteristic that may have influenced our respondents more, for example, than parental pressure to conform to religious norms. We may very well have a situation here of the sons reflecting what their fathers do (or did) rather than what their fathers said; put another way, in this case, actions appear to speak louder than words.

Friends' Expectations (Step 2)

The next most powerful variable is friends' expectations (derived from the

Index of Jewish Expectations). As we explained previously, peer influence is an important independent factor in the process of socialization to Jewish identification. While probably the most unrelated to father's religiosity of all our factors, friends' expectations still mildly depresses the relative contribution of father's religiosity. (Beta dropped from .33 to .29.) Peer contact and interaction are to some extent influenced by parents even during adolescence. We would expect, therefore, that one of the ways that father's religiosity affects Jewish identification is through its effect on the respondent's choice of peers and, hence, indirectly on peer expectations. It is interesting to note that the Index of Jewish Activities with Friends, which was significantly related to the JI Scale, does not make a significant independent contribution to the explanation of Jewish identification. This finding reflects the fact that friends' expectations is defined in terms of significant others whereas Jewish activities with friends includes all peers. Rosen, in his discussion of the influence of the peer group in shaping adolescent Jewish religiosity, emphasized the psychological relationship of the individual to the group in contrast to the objective behavior (1965: 95-96). This explanation would appear to be pertinent here as well.

Jewish Education (Step 3)

Following father's religiosity and friends' expectations, the third most important factor for Jewish identification was the extent of Jewish education. This means that the relationship between these two variables is not merely the result of parental or family characteristics; parents simultaneously influence their children by shaping Jewish identification and demanding participation in Jewish education. In addition, we may note that the beta value for friends' expectations remains stable at .25, suggesting that this variable is not influenced by Jewish education. Thus, it seems that the importance of Jewish education does not rest in the fact that it is an extension of parental power or peer pressure but that, through intellectual content and interpersonal relationships, it influences what a Jew should know, feel, and do. This would be particularly true when Jewish education extends well into adolescence, a key stage in the formation of the attitudes which constitute Jewish identification.

Other Family Factors (Steps 4-6)

Several other variables relating to the family experience of the respondents during adolescence made significant independent contributions to the explanation of Jewish identification. As indicated in table 5-1, these variables include activities with parents (derived from the Index of Jewish Activities) the presence of an older brother, and family expectations (derived from the Index of Jewish Expectations). The addition of each one of these variables depresses the independent effect of father's religiosity on the JI Scale from an initial beta value of .33 to a final value of .19 (see step 6). This appears to indicate that friends' expectations is the single most powerful independent effect on Jewish identification. But analytically it is more helpful to think in terms of types of factors rather than specific measures. Thus, the examination of the R^2 Change column in table 5-1 shows 18 percent of the variance explained by family variables, with 6 percent by friends' expectations and 4 percent by Jewish education.

What This Regression Analysis Tells Us

These findings are pertinent to understanding a common yet significant phenomenon of contemporary Jewish life: a family joining a synagogue when its child is of school age so that the child may develop a Jewish identification. While Jewish education has some independent effect on shaping Jewish identification and is not to be dismissed lightly, it represents only one dimension in the network of socialization factors involved in this process. More important, the child is going to look to his parents and to their behavior, to the expectations they hold, and, if he is a boy, particularly to his father (and even to his older brother if one is present), as a model for his own sense of Jewish identification. Thus, in such a situation where the significance of interpersonal contact with family and friends supersedes the role of Jewish education, the effect of the religious school in shaping Jewish identification will be mild but lasting (Shapiro and Dashefsky, 1974). Indeed, this may be the conscious intention of many parents: to produce a minimal amount of Jewish identification in their children ("just enough so he'll know he's Jewish"). For Jewish education to be more effective, the child has to see the utility of Jewish education in his family life, in what the family members do and say.

The implication, moreover, of the importance of the variable of friends' expectations in shaping Jewish identification is to focus on whether or not young people are supported by their friends regarding Jewish activities and attitudes created both at home and in the Jewish school. The type of situations in which peer group influence can operate may range from the informal context (attending religious services in the company of friends) to the formal context (membership in a Jewish youth organization). Although our measure does not indicate the exact nature of friends' expectations, we would expect that if they are congruent with those learned at home and in the school, they will represent a more powerful influence.

Father's JI Scale Score

To assess the independent effect of the father's attitudes, we relied on the ninety-eight pairs of fathers and sons for whom we have information. By taking the JI Scale score from the father's questionnaire, we were able to measure the effect of each of the scores of the fathers on the scores of their sons. The correlation between the JI Scales was .29, a significant yet, in terms of our expectations, low association. It appears again that a behavioral variable (father's religiosity) is a more powerful determinant of Jewish identification than an attitudinal variable (father's JI Scale score). In order to ascertain the contribution of the father's Jewish identification scale score to the explanation of Jewish identification among the younger men in our study, we carried out a regression analysis which added the father's JI Scale score to the socialization variables already found (in the analysis of all sons, N = 173) to have independent explanatory power. We found that the multiple correlation of these variables to the JI Scale was .55, about the same as the multiple correlation for the socialization variables, without the fathers' JI Scale scores ($R = .53$).

While the father's Jewish identification did have an independent effect on Jewish identification among the younger men in our regression analysis of the ninety-eight pairs (beta = .20), this contribution was, so to speak, "at the expense" of the other "father" variable, father's religiosity. In the analysis of all the sons ($N = 173$) father's religiosity has a beta weight of .19 in step 6 (table 5-1); in the ninety-eight pairs' analysis the beta weight of this variable is .08. It appears then that the addition of the father's JI Scale variable for the most part simply breaks up the independent contribution of father's influence into two variables. The total proportion of the variance explained by the inclusion of the father's JI Scale scores with the other socialization variables (30 percent for N=98) remains about the same as that which we already found for all younger men (28 percent for N=173). This finding suggests that further specification of attributes of the father or the family which might be associated with Jewish identification would probably add little, in terms of amount of variance accounted for, to our explanation of socialization to Jewish identification.

We have specified, then, a number of socialization factors, each of which has an independent effect on the variance in Jewish identification. In order of importance they are family (taken as one set of variables), friends, and Jewish education. Furthermore, our analysis indicates the interdependence of these socialization factors. Not only can we see the direct effect of these variables, but we also note the influence of these factors on one another, thus creating indirect influences as well; for example, father's religiosity appears to influence Jewish identification through its effect on friends' expectations, as well as in other ways.

Structural Effects

It is not our intent to argue that Jewish identification is solely a function of experiences during the formative adolescent years with family and friends and in the school. Indeed, we can explain more than one-fourth the variance in Jewish identification in terms of socialization factors. But what of the remaining three-quarters? It is our view that the experiences of childhood and adolescence lay the foundation for subsequent attitudes in adulthood, but that these attitudes are subject to modification and change by the ways in which the individual is integrated into the structure of his community and society. The individual's position in the social structure partly governs the range of behavior in which he may engage, which in turn affect the attitudes he holds.

Newman has suggested that there are two basic structural dimensions in society: (1) the vertical (based on social rewards), which consists of the economic, political, and educational institutions and (2) the horizontal (based on social space), which consists of residential, recreational, religious and (current) familial factors (1973: 129). In the data available to us we were able to examine the effects on Jewish identification of three sets of structural factors that described the respondents' current position in the community: residence, socioeconomic status and religiosity. Moreover, through the technique of regression analysis we can determine the relative independent effects of socialization vs. structural variables in the explanation of Jewish identification.

Socioeconomic Status

It is commonly assumed that socioeconomic status is a key variable affecting a host of factors related to aspects of ethnicity: friendship patterns, participation in voluntary associations, religiosity, denominational preference, and ethnic group identification. Ianni, in examining the relationship between socioeconomic status and ethnic identification among college-age youth has summarized what we should expect.

Generally the degree of ethnicity and group identification seems to be inversely related to socioeconomic status among college-level Jewish teenagers . . . As social mobility brings the Jewish teenager into increasing contact with the dominant American middle-class teenage culture, ethnicity diminishes (1964: 234).

Three indicators of socioeconomic status were measured: occupation, education, and income. (See Methodological Appendix for the operationalization of these variables.) An examination of the correlation coefficients for the JI Scale with occupation and with education (table 5-2)

Table 5-2

Zero-Order Coefficients Between JI Scale and Possible Structural Determinants

(Sons)

Possible Structural Determinants	Correlation with JI Scale
Socioeconomic Status	
Occupation	−.07
Income	.18[a]
Education	−.12
Residence	
Jewish Area	.03
Proportion of Neighbors	.10
Religiosity	
Synagogue Attendance	.46[a]
Synagogue Membership	.33[a]

[a]Significant at $P < .05$ for $N = 169$. All other coefficients not significant.

suggests the plausibility of Ianni's contention, although the relationship fails to reach statistical significance. In both cases there is a weak inverse correlation (Occupation, $r = -.07$; Education, $r = -.12$). More interesting than this weak association is the *positive* significant correlation between income and the JI Scale ($r = .18$). This unexpected finding stands up in the regression analysis to be discussed in a later section.

Perhaps income for this younger generation of men in their twenties measures something different than structural integration into the socioeconomic hierarchy. One possible explanation is that it reflects the number of children one has. It may be that among American Jews individuals with more income decide on the basis of family planning to have more children, which in turn stimulates a concern for education and participation in the Jewish community. Such a parental concern might heighten Jewish identification. However, subsequent analysis showed no statistically significant relationship between the number of children or the number of school-age children and Jewish identification.

There is another possible explanation as to why income is significantly related to the JI Scale. The amount of income derives mainly from one's occupation. Perhaps, among this younger generation group those who have lower incomes are for the most part still enrolled in college and are, therefore, more insulated from participation in and identification with the ethnic community. We would expect their behavior and attitudes to be governed more by the universalistic standards of the university. In contrast, those who have higher incomes have probably left college and taken permanent jobs. In these circumstances these individuals may seek out a familiar communal environment, one which they know. This environment may very well be the Jewish community they knew in their formative years and in which their parents, relatives, and some friends still participate. Hence, we would expect those men already employed to score higher on the JI Scale than those still in school. In order to test this hypothesis we recoded our occupation variable into two categories: those in school and those employed. We found as we expected that the recoded occupation variable was significantly associated with the level of income ($r = .47$) and with the score on the JI Scale ($r = .19$). The question then remains as to whether this occupation variable should replace the income variable in our regression analysis. We deal with this issue in our discussion of that analysis.

Residence

Sebald has succinctly summarized the argument for looking at residence as a structural effect on Jewish identification. While he was concerned with the relationship for adolescents, it seems likely that it would apply to adults as well.

The new ecological conditions [suburban migration], where Jews and Gentiles increasingly live next door to each other, have contributed to the blurring of formerly distinct outlines of the Jewish community in more than merely ecological terms—they have also blurred the psychological outlines. There are no longer as many close Jewish neighbors as there used to be to reinforce each other in respect to the observance of religious and subcultural rituals and holidays (1968:293).

Two measures of residential patterns were utilized: one variable specified whether or not the respondent lived in St. Paul's primary area of Jewish residence, Highland Park. It is important to keep in mind that while this area had the greatest concentration of Jewish residents, Jews still constituted a minority of the area's population. The categories of the variable "Jewish area" are living in Highland Park or living elsewhere. The correlation between Jewish area and the JI Scale was not significant ($r = .03$, table 5-2). The second residential variable aimed at measuring the respondent's perception of the proportion of Jews in his neighborhood by leaving the concept of neighbors undefined. Thus, proportion of neighbors Jewish was classified as none, few, about half, most, all, or nearly all. The correlation between this variable and the JI Scale was also not significant ($r = .10$, table 5-2).

Thus, it appears that the neighborhood in which one lives as an adult has no significant effect on Jewish identification. What is probably more significant for adults is not the physical proximity to other Jews but the social distance. We suggest, therefore, that the interpersonal dimension (the number of close friends who are Jewish) will probably be more significant than the ecological dimension (residence). Unfortunately, our data were confined primarily to the interpersonal influences in adolescence. Hence, we do not have a measure on such influences, e.g., friendship patterns for young adults.

Religiosity

The question of the role of religiosity in affecting Jewish group identification has been probed by philosophers as well as social scientists. Kenneth Stern, a philosopher who rejects Judaism but affirms his Jewishness, puts the issue in these terms:

I have already suggested, to adapt a well-known advertising slogan, "You don't have to be religious to be Jewish." But there is a related question that needs asking. If an individual Jew need not be religious and wants to remain a Jew, can he? Can Jewish identity survive without religion? In other words, can Judaism as a group phenomenon survive the passing of religious belief? If religious belief is discarded, it may well be argued that what eventually will happen is . . . the consequent loss of identity. According to this argument religious belief of some kind is the psychological foundation of Jewish identity and community. Even if religion is not requisite for the *individual* Jew, it is necessary for the maintenance of the group. Only as long as there is a Jewish ethnic group can the individual, although not religious, retain his Jewish identity (1969:197).

Stern himself is less concerned with the truth of this social psychological hypothesis than with its ethical implications for himself as a secular Jew. Marshall Sklare has also dealt with this question of the significance of religion for Jews as an ethnic community. He argues that Judaism can be viewed as an "ethnic church," in which both ethnicity and religiosity are articulated. According to Sklare, America's Jews prefer to be regarded as members of a religious group. Yet most have "wider Jewish interests than simply religion (or even possess other Jewish interests which serve to replace religion), but they feel nonetheless that—given American traditions—*religion must become the main expression of Jewish identification as well as the guarantor of Jewish ethnic survival*" (1969:110).

In order to empirically test the hypothesis of the relationship between religious factors and ethnic group identification, two measures of religiosity were utilized: the frequency of synagogue attendance and the degree of traditionalism in synagogue membership. Synagogue attendance was measured by the individual's response to the statement: "I usually attend synagogue services." Possible responses were: never, High Holidays only, occasionally, weekly, or daily. The correlation between synagogue attendance and the JI Scale was quite strong ($r = .46$, table 5-2). In fact, it was the variable most highly correlated with the JI Scale. The degree of traditionalism of synagogue membership was measured by the following categories: not a member, Reform, Conservative, or Orthodox. The correlation between synagogue membership and the JI Scale was also statistically significant ($r = .33$, see table 5-2).

A separate regression analysis for the structural variables confirmed the significance of synagogue attendance, synagogue membership, and income in that order for their independent effects in explaining the variance in the JI Scale (respective beta weights in the third and last step were: .38, .21, and .15). These factors taken together yield a multiple R of .52, which represents 27 percent of the variance explained. It should be recalled that the variance explained by the combined effect of the socialization variables was 28 percent.

Socialization Effects vs. Structural Effects

We have discussed the key variables, for which data were available, that describe the respondents' current characteristics and their effects on Jewish identification. Now we can compare the relative effects of socialization experiences and present structural factors.

Certainly these two aspects of social life are not mutually exclusive. The sociological approach necessitates considering past and present social experiences. Hence, there exists a combination of socialization and social structure analyses within a sociological social psychology. While appreciating that each person acts and thinks as a function of both his social biography and the present social environment, many empirical studies actually seem to argue for an "either-or" approach by dealing only with one or the other set of variables. Here we juxtapose socialization and structural effects in order to: (1) specify as far as possible the differing effects of both past and present social life on individuals, particularly on Jewish identification; (2) indicate something of the complex interrelationships between these two types of factors; and (3) show that the power of sociological explanation is increased when both socialization and social structure variables are taken into consideration. The combined effects of the socialization and structural factors that make significant independent contributions to the explanation of Jewish identification produced a multiple correlation coefficient, $R = .63$. Thus, our socialization and structural variables taken together account for 40 percent of the variance in the JI Scale (table 5-3, step 8).

What does it indicate when changes in our entire set of variables account for less than half of the changes in the dependent variable? The appropriate reply might seem to be: "Not much." We do not agree. It means a great deal. Given the countless factors that may affect any complex aspect of human behavior and the difficulties in specifying and measuring such factors, a multiple R of .63 in explaining Jewish identification (accounting for 40 percent of the variance) *is a very important finding*.

While we have already indicated the types of issues that we can explore by juxtaposing socialization and structural variables, the data in table 5-3, which is a summary of our regression analysis, allows us to specifically answer several questions: (1) Which particular variables are most important? (2) What effect does the introduction of a new variable have on the independent effects of other variables? (3) What is the relative contribution of socialization variables versus structural variables?

The Effects of Religiosity

The hypothesis articulated by both Sklare and Stern that religion operates to sustain ethnic identification among Jews is supported by our data. The single most important variable is the current frequency of synagogue attendance (beta = .46). This variable has the highest zero-order correlation with Jewish identification and, therefore, is entered first in our regression equation (see step 1). Moreover, throughout succeeding stages of analysis (steps 2 through 8) it remains about twice as important as any other single variable (i.e., its beta weight is generally twice as large as the beta weight of any other variable). Finally, we note that the degree of traditionalism of current synagogue membership is equally as important as any other single remaining variable (beta weights in steps 3 to 8).

Our findings bear striking similarity to those reported by Lazerwitz in comparing current attitudes and involvement in the Jewish community with socialization factors for a sample of Chicago Jews (1971). Religious behavior had the strongest direct effect on a number of dimensions of Jewish life. Similar findings for a sample of Israeli high-school students were reported by Herman:

The degree of religious observance is the crucial variable in the study of Jewish identity. Significant differences consistently appear on Jewish identity items between religious, traditionalist, and non-religious students . . . Not only do the religious students feel more Jewish and value their Jewishness more under all circumstances, but they feel closer to, and have a greater sense of identification with, Jews everywhere (1970:115).

Family Influences

The second most powerful variable in explaining Jewish identification is family expectations (derived from the Index of Jewish Expectations) with a beta weight of .24. The independent contribution of family expectations gradually decreases as other related family and socialization variables are introduced (steps 3 through 8). One striking difference in comparing the socialization effects (table 5-1) to the combined effects of socialization and structural variables (table 5-3) is the position of family expectations (from the last step in table 5-1 to the second step in table 5-3). In other words, family expectations replaces father's religiosity (which shifts from the first step in table 5-1 to the last step in table 5-3) as the most important socialization variable. It appears that the effects of father's religiosity on the JI Scale are likely to be indirect, operating through such current structural variables as synagogue attendance and synagogue membership. This can be seen as a two-step process: first, father's religiosity accounting in part for synagogue attendance and synagogue membership; and second, the two variables being among the most important determinants of variation in the JI Scale. Since family expectations and father's religiosity are significantly interrelated ($r = .32$), some of the effect of family influence is represented in the independent contribution of father's religiosity. When this contribution is attenuated (beta = .12 in step 8) for the reason just discussed, the independent effect of family expectations becomes more important. We would expect such a factor to be a strong determinant of Jewish identification given the importance of the family in shaping attitudes and values.

Another interesting difference in comparing socialization effects (table 5-1) with the combined effects (table 5-3) is the elimination of activities with parents (derived from the Index of Jewish Activities) as a significant variable in the explanation of Jewish identification. Many family expectations in adolescence become internalized and remain as relatively enduring attitudes. Adolescent activities with parents appear to become less important for one's attitudes as more current activities (e.g., synagogue attendance and synagogue membership) supersede them.

Lastly, under the rubric of family influences we observe the persistent significant independent effect of having an older brother. Since this was more or less a serendipitous finding, we have not been able to further explore its implications. Ultimately we need more data on the characteristics of the older brother and his relationship to the respondent to support the role-model hypothesis we would advance in dealing with this issue. It appears that our interest in family influences in shaping ethnic identification suggests not only the significance of parents but of siblings as well.

Table 5-3
Stepwise Multiple Regression Analysis; Socialization and Structural Determinants of Jewish Identification (Sons)

Step	Independent Variable	Beta Weight	F Ratio	Multiple R	R^2	R^2 Change
1	Synagogue Attendance	.46	45.5	.46	.21	.21
2	Synagogue Attendance	.43	42.1	.52	.27	.06
	Family Expectations (IJE)	.24	12.8			
3	Synagogue Attendance	.38	30.5	.55	.30	.03
	Family Expectations (IJE)	.22	11.0			
	Synagogue Membership	.19	7.2			
4	Synagogue Attendance	.36	27.6	.57	.33	.03
	Family Expectations (IJE)	.20	9.5			
	Synagogue Membership	.20	8.5			
	Jewish Education	.17	8.6			
5	Synagogue Attendance	.35	27.8	.59	.35	.02
	Family Expectations (IJE)	.19	9.0			
	Synagogue Membership	.19	7.9			
	Jewish Education	.17	6.7			
	Income	.15	5.8			

6	Synagogue Attendance	.32	22.5			
	Family Expectations (IJE)	.17	7.3			
	Synagogue Membership	.18	7.3			
	Jewish Education	.17	7.2			
	Income	.15	5.4			
	Friends' Expectations (IJE)	.15	5.3	.61	.37	.02
7	Synagogue Attendance	.31	21.9			
	Family Expectations (IJE)	.17	7.3			
	Synagogue Membership	.16	5.6			
	Jewish Education	.14	5.1			
	Income	.15	5.8			
	Friends' Expectations (IJE)	.15	5.6			
	Older Brother	.13	3.8	.62	.39	.02
8	Synagogue Attendance	.28	16.1			
	Family Expectations (IJE)	.14	4.5			
	Synagogue Membership	.14	4.2			
	Jewish Education	.14	4.8			
	Income	.15	5.8			
	Friends' Expectations	.15	5.7			
	Older Brother	.12	3.5			
	Father's Religiosity	.12	2.7	.63	.40	.01

Note: All F ratios significant with $DF = 1$, 167 in step 1 and $DF = 8$, 160 in step 8.

Jewish Education

The persistence of Jewish education as a significant variable supports our contention of its "mild but lasting effect" on Jewish identification. It is not one of the major independent factors, but its contribution remains fairly stable (steps 4 to 8) with the introduction of each of four additional variables. Our data indicate little interrelation (in terms of statistically significant correlations) between Jewish education and other explanatory variables, both socializational and structural. Jewish education appears to be an isolable independent entity affecting Jewish identification. In this regard mention should be made of the relatively unique nature of Jewish education in the community where this study took place. Whereas in most communities each synagogue congregation operates its own religious school, in St. Paul the community as a whole supports one central nonideological school, The Talmud Torah, with congregations offering a minimal supplementary religious education. This homogeneity in Jewish education may explain the lack of association we found between this variable and such socialization effects as activities with parents or structural effects like synagogue membership. In other words, variations in family activities and attitudes might not have as much an effect on the amount of Jewish education attained in St. Paul as in those places where parental attitudes are perhaps more important in determining the type and extent of Jewish education. For instance, Lazerwitz (1971) finds for a sample of Chicago Jews a correlation of $r = .31$ between childhood background and Jewish education compared to a correlation of .05 between activities with parents and Jewish education among our respondents. Furthermore, since among St. Paul's young Jewish men the type and extent of Jewish education is more of a constant than in many other Jewish communities, we would not expect Jewish education in adolescence to account for as much of the variation in current participation in the Jewish community as is measured, for instance, by synagogue attendance. Again comparing our data to that of Lazerwitz, he finds that among his respondents Jewish education and religious behavior were significantly related ($r = .36$), while we find that Jewish education and synagogue attendance are not significantly associated ($r = .12$).

Finally, it is possible that the homogeneity of the distribution of Jewish education among our respondents depresses the effect of this variable on Jewish identification. In another community where there are higher proportions of individuals with very high or very low amounts of Jewish education, it is likely the variable of Jewish education would have a stronger effect on variations in Jewish identification.

Income

As we indicated earlier in this chapter, we suspected that the unexpected direct relationship between income and the JI Scale represented something other than merely socioeconomic status. We suggested it might reflect whether the individual was still enrolled in school or employed fulltime. Hence, we carried out a separate regression analysis replacing income with this recoded measure of occupation to see if this enhanced the power of our explanation of Jewish identification. The resulting beta weight for occupation (recoded) was not significant, indicating that we should keep income in our analysis. This variable, however, may still reflect in part whether the respondent was in school and influenced by the college community or was employed fulltime and possibly more involved in the ethnic community. (Income and this recoded measure of occupation were strongly associated, $r = .47$.)

More than this, however, income probably reflects the type of occupation one has. The more traditional Jewish occupations (managing a family-owned business or practicing medicine or law) would tend to be more financially lucrative. These occupations are more likely to bind the individual more closely to his family of orientation and to the Jewish community. In contrast, working in a bureaucratized profession is less financially rewarding. Such employment attenuates the ties to family and community because the worker is less able to control his own occupational career and must be more responsive to the demands of his employer, including possibly moving from one city to another. However, probably the most important characteristic of most bureaucratic occupations is that they bring the individual in contact with members of the community at large rather than with the members of his ethnic community. For instance, the Jewish physician in private practice is likely to draw a significant number of his patients from the local Jewish community, whereas the Jewish physician employed at a county hospital will have as his patients a cross-section of the larger community. Similar contrasts apply to the private-practicing lawyer in comparison to a member of the corporate legal staff.

This interpretation is consistent with our illustration in chapter 3 concerning the Silversmiths, a father and son pair in our sample. They were among the five highest scorers on the JI Scale. The younger Mr. Silversmith was the only young man among the five. He was described as attending college but not having graduated. Most relevant, however, is the fact that he was employed in the family business and was in the highest third of the income distribution, earning over $12,000. (The recoded occupation variable may only be applicable for the age cohort of men in their twenties, since the student vs. full-time employment distinction is usually confined to this age group.)

Finally, in looking at table 5-3 we note that the beta value of income remains the same (.15) from step 5, when it is first introduced, to the last step, 8. This means that income is relatively unaffected by other variables introduced subsequently in the analysis.

Past and Present Behavior

In summarizing the relative effects of past socialization experiences and present structural characteristics (see table 5-3 and particularly the R^2 Change column) we find that all of the five socialization variables explain 14 percent of the variance in Jewish identification, while the three structural variables explain 26 percent of the variance. Although this finding suggests the primacy of structural over socialization effects, we cannot completely separate past and present behavior. The individual is a unitary organism with an evolving life history and an evaluating sense of history. In other words, one's past experiences are an integral part of one's present behavior. This characteristic is illustrated by the fact that such socialization variables as father's religiosity, friends' expectations, and activities with parents were related significantly to current behavior: synagogue attendance and synagogue membership. Here socialization experiences operate indirectly on Jewish identification by affecting current religiosity.

We interpret our data to indicate that Jewish identification is determined by a complex array of factors, some more interrelated than others, but all constituting a network of experiences, activities, and associations. Our sociological approach to ethnic identification led us to specify and measure certain variables within the period of adolescent socialization. However, our data indicate that these variables operate for the most part indirectly through their effect on current structural factors that in turn influence Jewish identification. The socialization experiences that we have described lay the foundation for later adult activities and attributes that are important in shaping Jewish identification.

The central theme of this chapter is aptly illustrated in an encounter between one of our colleagues and his father. The colleague was a professor at a university located in a small town that had no synagogue. He had been raised in Brooklyn in a very traditionally Jewish manner by his parents. During his late adolescence and young adulthood he had drifted away from the traditionalism of his parents even though he remained actively committed to Jewish peoplehood. His father came to visit him in the small, rural college town. As they were taking a leisurely walk the father said quietly,

"The house is lovely; the surroundings are beautiful; the air is clean and healthful . . . but my son, do you want to be a Jew? Leave!" Our colleague did not wait for us to publish the results of our study. He now lives in Israel.

Summary

In this chapter we present the heart of our study of the determinants of Jewish identification: a regression analysis of socialization effects and structural effects, considered separately and then combined.

The socialization variables taken together are correlated with the JI Scale at $R = .53$. This means that these factors in combination account for 28 percent (i.e., the square of .53) of the variance in our Jewish identification measure. Our regression analysis allows us to see the independent contribution of each variable to the total variance explained. The final socialization variables regression equation indicates that family variables account for 18 percent of the variance; friend's expectations, 6 percent; and Jewish education, 4 percent. Of the family variables, father's religiosity appears to be the most powerful single factor. While regression analysis indicates the independent effects of each of the socialization variables, it also indicates the interdependence of these factors. Thus, father's religiosity influences Jewish identification through its effect on friend's expectations, as well as directly.

While emphasizing adolescent experiences, we have included in our analysis three sets of factors which allow us to assess certain aspects of our respondents' current position. These "structural" factors are socioeconomic status, residence, and religiosity. Of the variables used to measure these factors, the following were significantly correlated with the JI Scale: income ($r = .18$), synagogue attendance ($r = .46$) and synagogue membership ($r = .33$). These variables taken together correlated with the JI Scale at $R = .52$, which means they accounted for 27 percent of the variance in our measure of Jewish identification.

Finally, both socialization and structural variables were combined. The effects of all such variables (those that made significant independent contributions to accounting for variance in the JI Scale) yielded a multiple correlation coefficient of $R = .63$, which accounts for 40 percent of the variance in Jewish identification. Our regression analysis of these eight variables indicates that in the final solution the five socialization variables account for 14 percent of the variance, while the three structural variables explain 26 percent of the variance in Jewish identification. This suggests the primacy of structural factors over socialization effects. However, the data indicate that socialization factors have an indirect impact on Jewish identification by affecting current religiosity. In sum, adolescent experiences provide a foundation for later adult activities which are manifestly central in shaping and maintaining one's Jewish identification.

6

The Older Generation: Comparisons and Contrasts with the Younger Generation

In chapter 3 we concluded that since significant differences existed between the generations of younger and older men in aspects of Jewish identification, it was useful to proceed in terms of separate analyses for each generation. We found that the older men scored significantly higher on the JI Scale than the younger men, and that in some related areas of Jewish beliefs and attitudes the differences were even greater than in the overall JI Scale. Similarly, Lazerwitz in his study of Chicago Jews found:

that there has been a substantial, and statistically significant increase in the percentage of Jewish men ranking low in overall Jewish identification from the first generation to the third generation. However, a much more complicated picture emerges when . . . more specific identity indices are carefully examined (1970: 53).

Lazerwitz goes on to show that "there is, indeed, a substantial increase in the percentages ranking low on the indices measuring religious behavior . . . and Jewishness of the childhood home."

By contrast Lazerwitz points out that differences were not nearly as great for the variable of Jewish education. What these data suggest is that in the course of examining the similarities and differences between the generations we should not make the simplistic assumption that the same variables are operating to produce Jewish identification for the older men as operated for the younger men—only more so. Rather, a more complex comparison is likely to emerge along the lines suggested by Lazerwitz.

There is one limitation to our data in this chapter that we should point out. In many cases the recollections of the fathers of their adolescent experiences were based on events that took place thirty or more years before. Undoubtedly some of the respondents had difficulty in recalling the important persons and events of this time period. Hence, for some of our possible antecedent variables some fathers did not provide the needed information on the questionnaire.

Toward a Jewish Socialization Syndrome

In developing our explanation of the determinants of Jewish identification for the older generation, we will limit ourselves to a comparison with the younger generation. The basic theoretical foundations for most of the

Table 6-1
Zero-Order Correlation Coefficients Between JI Scale and Possible Socialization Determinants
(Fathers)

Possible Socialization Determinants	Correlation with JI Scale
Family	
Index of Jewish Expectations (IJE)	.34
Index of Jewish Activities (IJA: with Parents)	.11[a]
Older Brother (Presence)	−.05[a]
Father	
Religiosity	.29
Knowledge of Perspective	.28
Perceived Similarity of Perspective	.23
Peers	
Index of Jewish Expectations (IJE)	.20
Index of Jewish Activities (IJA)	.27
Jewish Education	.24

Note: Correlation coefficients were significant for $r = .19$, at $p < .05$ with $N = 107$.
[a]Not significant.

variables used here has already been developed in chapters 4 and 5. We shall discuss both the findings of the correlation analysis presented in table 6-1 (see table 4-1 for sons) and the regression analysis presented in table 6-2 (see table 5-1 for sons) for the various agents of socialization.

Our goal here is not a restatement of theory and data presented in previous chapters with a new population. Rather, we are concerned with highlighting the important commonalities and differences in the determinants of Jewish identification for the two generations of American Jews in question. We turn first to a comparison of influences in the family.

Family

1. *Activities with parents is not significantly related to Jewish identification in the case of the fathers* ($r = .11$).
2. *Family expectations is significantly associated with the JI Scale for fathers* ($r = .34$) *as well as sons.* Unlike the case of the sons (chapter 5) where we argued that overt behavior (father's religiosity) was a more powerful influence than parental pressure (family expectations), in the case of the fathers the latter is more powerful than overt behavior (activities with parents, which has no significant effect). It appears that, over the longer

period of time, which has elapsed since the fathers' adolescence, the influence of a behavioral characteristic like activities with parents has become insignificant, while on the cognitive level family expectations persists as a significant variable. (See chapter 5 on friends' expectations.)

3. *The presence of an older brother is not significantly related to Jewish identification for members of the older generation* $(r = -.05)$. This finding points up the greater influence of siblings in shaping Jewish identification among the generation of sons. This may best be understood by relating it to the attenuated control and influence of parents over their children in the more recent past, accompanied by a rising influence of peers. Thus, in the case of the younger generation, an older brother may facilitate the respondent's integration into the network of peer activities and influences, which is now more important in shaping Jewish identification than it was during the fathers' adolescence.

For the fathers' generation the family appears to have been *the* reference group. Family continues to be a fundamental reference group for the younger generation, but through its members (older brother) it also brings the individual into other communication channels (Shibutani, 1955). Within the family, the father appears to have been the primary significant other vis-à-vis influence on Jewish identification. Nevertheless, we note some important generational differences in how this influence is manifested.

The Father

4. *There is a significant relationship between:* (a) *the respondent's knowledge of,* or (b) *perceived similarity to his father's perspective and Jewish identification* $(r = .28, r = .23,$ respectively). Neither of these variables was related to the JI Scale for the sons. The importance of considering these variables for the fathers depends to a great extent on some differences in family backgrounds surrounding the socialization experiences of these two generations. Data on two characteristics suggest that the father was less likely to be present in the case of the older men. One measure tells us the proportion in each generation who were immigrants (older generation: 9 percent; younger generation: 3 percent), which means that those respondents were probably the first to arrive in the U.S. and, therefore, came without their fathers. The other measure gives us the proportion in each generation whose fathers were deceased when the respondent was an adolescent (older generation: 18 percent; younger generation: 10 percent). Therefore, when the father was present, knowledge of and similarity to father's perspective together indicate the effect of close father-son ties on Jewish identification.

Knowledge of father's perspective was measured by a four-point Likert scale measuring the strength of agreement (strongly agree, agree, disagree, strongly disagree) with the statement, "I knew how my father stood on most issues." As previously mentioned, this item was significantly correlated with the JI Scale. Perceived similarity to father's perspective was similarly measured utilizing the following statement, "My father and I had the same general outlook." As we have seen, this item was also significantly correlated with the JI Scale. These relationships exist in the case of the older generation but not the younger one because they reflect in part the greater variation of the presence of the father among the former and hence the greater variation in the capacity of the father to serve as a role-model and mold the Jewish identification of his son.

This finding is borne out in the regression analysis in which knowledge of father's perspective has a significant independent effect on the JI Scale score, with an initial beta weight of .24 (table 6-2, step 3). The variable perceived similarity to father's perspective is not included in the equation because its effects, at least in part, *have already been absorbed by the preceding variable*. To a certain extent a "halo effect" may be operating in the case of members of the older generation, most of whose fathers were deceased. Their veneration of their fathers may have led them toward a greater perceived similarity between their own perspective and that of their fathers, which undoubtedly included a strong Jewish identification. Hence, perceived similarity to their father's perspective would undoubtedly be positively related to their own Jewish identification.

5. *Family expectations appears as most important and father's religiosity as least important in the case of the older generation, reversing the pattern of the younger generation* (table 6-2). As table 6-1 indicates, the correlation coefficient for family expectations is slightly larger ($r = .34$) than for father's religiosity ($r = .29$). These values determine the initial variable in the regression equation, with family expectations preceding father's religiosity (see table 6-2, step 4) although their beta values reach the same level (.21).

As we indicated in chapter 5, the effects of one variable have partially been absorbed by the other, producing this first and last combination of the two variables in both generations. Here again we may have an example of the pre-eminence of perceived expectations over a behavioral characteristic during the long period of time that has elapsed since the fathers passed through adolescence. We now turn to the relative influence of other likely significant others, i.e., peers.

Peers

6. *There is a reversal of the pattern in the older generation with peer*

activities being more closely correlated to the JI Scale than peer expecta-tions ($r = .27$ and $r = .20$, respectively). This minor difference appears to contradict our previous statement with respect to the greater salience of expectations over activity as distance from the experiences increases, but, it probably reflects the crudeness of our measure, since for the older men these experiences occurred thirty to fifty years ago. Hence, 52 percent of the fathers reported no peer activities, compared with only 25 percent of the sons, and fully 62 percent of the fathers reported no peer expectations (from significant others) compared to 44 percent of the sons. What does remain, however, is a measure of peer influence whose significance may be assessed in the regression analysis. As in chapter 5, we find that the second most important independent effect on the JI Scale score is the measure of peer influence (in this case activities) with an initial beta weight of .25 (see table 6-2, step 2). Separate regression analyses were carried out for each generation assessing the relative effects of the expectation for participation in Jewish activities by the respondent's friends, his father, or his mother. In the case of the older generation, the order of importance as determined by the beta weights was mother's expectations (.22), father's expectations (.16), and friends expectations (.14). In the case of the younger generation, the results were: friends' expectations (.27), father's expectations (.20), and mother's expectations (.11). These results yield one other interesting finding aside from the shifting importance favoring peers over parents in the younger generation: the relative influence of the mother over the father is reversed in the younger generation. Thus, the prevailing assumption of the greater importance of the mother in shaping the religious and ethnic orientation of the child may have been an accurate assumption in the past, but may no longer be so.

Now we come to what perhaps is the most significant generational difference in socialization to Jewish identification.

Jewish Education

7. *Jewish education makes no significant independent contribution to the explanation of the JI Scale in the case of the older generation, whereas it does in the younger generation.* While Jewish education is significantly related to the JI Scale (table 6-1: $r = .24$) at about the same level as for the younger men, its beta weight is not significant. Thus, in the fathers' genera-tion the effects of Jewish education were not independent of those of the home. This is probably because in the older generation a formalized system of Jewish education was not extensive, and frequently such education was entrusted to a *melamed* (a tutor or teacher) who came to the student's home to give a private lesson rather than to the *heder* (the East European type of school). It was in the post World War Two period that increased assimila-

tion helped to produce a more formalized system of Jewish education for the younger generation. A comparison of the relationship between several of the socialization factors and Jewish education in both generations supports this notion. For example, in the younger generation no significant relationships existed between Jewish education and family expectations, father's Religiosity, peer expectations, or activities with parents. By contrast, among the older men Jewish education was significantly associated with, for example, family expectations (r = .20), father's religiosity (r = .30), and activities with friends (r = .21). Thus, the decline in the pervasiveness of the Jewish subculture as part of the pattern of acculturation in the generation of younger men has led to Jewish education having a significant independent effect on Jewish identification. For a different but related analysis that draws the same conclusion, see Dashefsky on "Interactions and identity: the Jewish case" (1970).

Summarizing the Socialization Syndrome

In the older generation the four variables reported in the regression analysis (step 4, table 6-2) account for 26 percent of the variance in Jewish identification, roughly equivalent to the 28 percent for the six variables reported for the sons. While in the last step of the regression analysis the single most important variable is activities with friends (beta = .25), we should again deal with the family variables as one factor. In this way we see that the peer influence variable accounts for 6 percent of the variance (table 6-2, step 2) and the remaining family influence variables explain 20 percent of the variance.

What we see here in the microcosm of the Jewish experience that our two generations of respondents represent is the emergence of factors complementary to the one-time singular importance of the authority of elders in shaping Jewish identification. In the case of the fathers, who are primarily second generation, the independent influence of peers along with the family has been noted. In the case of the sons, who are primarily third generation, the independent influence of Jewish education along with the family and peers has been observed. We can only speculate on the possible further extension of this Jewish socialization syndrome in subsequent generations, e.g., the extent of informal education (Jewish camping, trips to Israel, etc.) or participation in voluntary organizations (religious fellowships and Zionist action groups).

The Continuity of Jewish Identification

We suggested in chapter 5 that a sequence of socialization experiences

Table 6-2
Stepwise Multiple Regression Analysis: Socialization Determinants of Jewish Identification (Fathers)

Step	Independent Variable	Beta Weight	F Ratio	Multiple R	R^2	R^2 Change
1	Family Expectations (IJE)	.33	12.4	.33	.11	.11
2	Family Expectations (IJE)	.31	11.7	.41	.17	.06
	Activities with Friends (IJA)	.25	7.7			
3	Family Expectations (IJE)	.28	9.1	.47	.22	.05
	Activities with Friends (IJA)	.25	8.0			
	Knowledge of Father's Perspective	.24	7.6			
4	Family Expectations (IJE)	.21	5.2	.51	.26	.04
	Activities with Friends (IJA)	.25	8.9			
	Knowledge of Father's Perspective	.21	5.7			
	Father's Religiosity	.21	5.3			

Note: All F ratios significant with $DF = 1$, 105 in step 1 to $DF = 4$, 102 in step 4.

Table 6-3
Zero-Order Correlation Coefficients (r) Between JI Scale and Possible Structural Determinants
(Fathers)

Possible Structural Determinants	Correlation with JI Scale
Residence	
Jewish Area	.21[a]
Proportion of Neighbors Jewish	.10
Socioeconomic Status	
Occupation	.08
Education	.10
Income	.07
Religiosity	
Synagogue Attendance	.45[a]
Synagogue Membership	.30[a]

[a]Significant at $p < .05$ for $N = 117$. All other coefficients not significant.

affects the individual's structural integration into the community, which in turn shapes Jewish identification. Thus far in this chapter we have compared the socialization experiences of our two generations. To complete the picture we need to contrast the fathers and sons with respect to their differences when both socialization and structural factors are analyzed. Again we shall focus on comparisons between the two generations. We shall discuss both the findings of the correlation analysis presented in table 6-3 (see table 5-2 for sons) and the regression analyses presented in table 6-4 (see table 5-3 for sons) in terms of the structural variables and of the comparison between socialization and structural effects.

Structural Effects

1. *Living in a Jewish area (i.e., Highland Park) was significantly associated with higher JI Scale scores in the fathers' generation ($r = .21$). (It was not in the sons' case.)* Unlike the younger men, the older ones have more established roots in the community both in terms of more extensive socialization experiences and structural factors like synagogue affiliation and residence. Unlike the younger men, they completed their advanced education a long time ago and do not see themselves as currently in a transitional stage. Nevertheless, the regression analysis in table 6-4 indi-

Table 6-4
Stepwise Multiple Regression Analysis: Socialization and Structural Determinants of Jewish Identification (Fathers)

Step	Independent Variable	Beta Weight	F Ratio	Multiple R	R^2	F^2 Change
1	Synagogue Attendance	.48	31.2	.48	.23	.23
2	Synagogue Attendance	.47	32.8	.54	.30	.07
	Activities with Friends (IJA)	.26	9.9			
3	Synagogue Attendance	.43	26.6	.57	.33	.03
	Activities with Friends (IJA)	.26	10.0			
	Knowledge of Father's Perspective	.19	5.1			
4	Synagogue Attendance	.38	19.9	.59	.35	.02
	Activities with Friends (IJA)	.25	9.4			
	Knowledge of Father's Perspective	.17	4.3			
	Family Expectations (IJE)	.16	3.5			

Note: All F ratios significant with $DF = 1,105$ in step 1 to $DF = 4, 102$ in step 4.

cates that the variable of Jewish area has no independent effect on the JI Scale score. An independent regression analysis of the three structural variables significantly associated with the JI Scale indicated that only synagogue attendance and Jewish area had significant beta weights (.43 and .15 respectively). Nevertheless, we note that the independent effect of synagogue attendance on Jewish indentification is nearly three times the effect of living in a Jewish area. With the addition of the socialization variables the independent effect of residence is eliminated.

The effects of living in a Jewish area apparently were picked up by the other variables in the equation. This suggests that at least in a community like St. Paul, where Jews do not constitute a majority in any neighborhood, residence is not important in shaping Jewish identification.

2. *Income is not significantly related to Jewish identification in the older generation (as it was in the younger one)*. In chapter 5 we indicated that the independent effect of the income variable tended in part to reflect an idiosyncratic characteristic of the younger men, the occupational status of student vs. full-time employment, with the latter encouraging increased involvement in the Jewish community. In the older generation this distinction no longer exists; hence, the effects of income on the JI Scale score are insignificant.

3. *Synagogue attendance has a significant independent effect on the JI Scale score, as in the younger generation, but synagogue membership does not*. In the case of the older generation there was less variability in terms of synagogue membership, with only 3 percent nonmembers compared to 18 percent among the younger men. Thus, we find that synagogue attendance is the most important structural variable that operates in both generations for reasons which we indicated in chapter 5 in our discussion of "The Effects of Religiosity." Synagogue attendance is the only structural factor to be included in the final regression analysis.

Socialization vs. Structural Effects

The combined effect of the four variables (three socialization variables and one structural variable) in the final regression solution produced a multiple correlation coefficient ($R = .59$) only slightly less than that produced with eight variables in the solution for the sons. These four factors account for 35 percent of the variance in the older generation's JI Scale scores. Similar to the case of the younger generation, we find among the older men the greater explanatory power of the structural factor, synagogue attendance. This variable accounted for 23 percent of the variance in Jewish identification compared to the 12 percent accounted for by the three socialization variables (see table 6-4: R^2 Change column). However, as in the sons' case, we should consider the effect of socialization experiences on current practices that are important in accounting for Jewish identification. We can see this by considering briefly some of the relationships in the final regression solution for the fathers' data and comparing this to the sons' case.

In the older generation, activities with friends makes a stronger independent contribution to Jewish identification than either family expectations or fathers' religiosity (which has no independent effect). (Compare table 5-3, step 8 to table 6-4, step 4). Comparing the generations, we find peer effects accounting for 7 percent of the variance among the older men and only 2 percent among the younger men. Further, in the older generation peer effects make a stronger independent contribution to the variance explained than family effects (family expectations). Why this unexpected reversal of expected findings?

The answer, perhaps, lies in part in considering the indirect as well as the direct effect of these socialization variables. Indicative of this is the stronger relationship between family expectations and synagogue attendance in the older generation ($r = .32$) compared to that found in the younger group ($r = .12$). This means that for the fathers a part of the effect of family expectations on Jewish identification takes place indirectly through the effect of family expectations on synagogue attendance, which in turn affects Jewish identification. The indirect effect is measured by subtracting the beta weight from the correlation coefficient; hence, the indirect effect of Family Expectation for Fathers is ($.33 - .15) = .18$, and for Sons it is ($.29 - .14) = .15$.) Further, this process, by diminishing the independent, direct effect of family expectations, raises the direct effect of activities with friends more for the fathers than it does for the sons. Finally, these relationships may be a function of the shifting saliency of the variables as the second generation grows older. Some of these relationships may yet appear in the third generation as its members grow older.

In summary, the general thrust of our findings in this chapter with respect to the fathers is similar to that of the sons. The major difference is that the range of factors included in the final step of the analysis for the sons (table 5-3) is much broader than that for the fathers (table 6-4). Most notable in the latter case is the lack of a significant independent effect of Jewish education, older brother, father's religiosity, and synagogue membership.

In the 1950s it was fashionable to interpret the "religious revival" of that era in terms of Hansen's law: a return by the grandchildren of immigrants to the ways of the grandparents which the parents themselves had discarded (Herberg, 1960). We began by noting Lazerwitz's cautionary statement about examining the variations in the different factors associated with Jewish identification. Lazerwitz concluded his article with a refutation of the simplistic notions of Hansen. We concur with this judgment and offer the evidence presented about these sons and fathers in support. The third generation is not as identified with the Jewish people, as is the second generation (although this might well increase in later stages of life), but for the younger men a more variegated set of factors appear to independently contribute to Jewish identification. This is what Judah J. Shapiro was alluding to:

The Jew no longer being produced in the home in the first years of life, the Jewish agencies take over the task . . . the prevailing communal activity . . .[is] Jew-making, as distinguished from a period when Jewish communal activity was maintained by those who were Jews to begin with (1970:12).

Summary

In this chapter the same analysis carried out in the previous two chapters is applied to the older generation. This analysis is much briefer, since we have already laid out our theoretical position and since we limit ourselves to comparing the data for the fathers' generation with our previous findings about the younger generation. In addition, many fewer variables remained in the final regression analysis for this chapter.

The regression analysis of socialization effects resulted in four variables in the final solution: family expectations, activities with friends, knowledge of father's perspective, and father's religiosity. These variables produce a multiple correlation coefficient with Jewish identification of $R = .51$, accounting, therefore, for about 26 percent of the variance. In contrast to the younger men's data, the following variables did *not* make an independent contribution to the variance in Jewish identification: activities with parents, older brother, and Jewish education. In addition, knowledge of father's perspective appears in the father's socialization regression analysis and not in the sons'. Overall, 20 percent of the variance in Jewish identification was accounted for by family variables and 6 percent by the peer influence variable.

Turning to a consideration of structural effects, the only variable that made an independent contribution in accounting for the variance in the JI Scale was synagogue attendance. (Synagogue attendance and Jewish identification were correlated at $r = .45$.) Further, in the final combined regression analysis this variable is by far the single most important factor in accounting for Jewish identification. It accounted for 23 percent of the variance compared to 12 percent for the three socialization variables combined. As in our discussion of the sons, however, we point out how socialization experiences can affect current practices, in this case synagogue attendance, which in turn is more directly related to Jewish identification. Our analysis indicated that there are important differences between the generations and that the younger men present, perhaps, even a more complex situation than the older generation.

7 The Shaping of Perspective: Consequences of Being Jewish

The recent social science literature shows an increasing interest (actually, reinterest) in phenomenological analysis. Books and articles appear carrying titles starting with "The Social Reality of ————," the "Social Meaning of ————," or "The Social Construction of ————." Such titles indicate the social scientist's concern with the social processes by which people's ideas, attitudes, beliefs, etc. are formed, as well as with the varying conceptions and perceptions of different social collectivities. On the psychiatric and currently popular level, R.D. Laing uses a phenomenological approach (1967); in terms of sociological theory there is the increasing popularity of a sociology of knowledge approach, especially the work of Berger and Luckmann (1966). A central concept in such an approach is "perspective," often used synonomously with orientation or outlook. Shibutani defines perspective as

an ordered view of one's world—what is taken for granted about the attributes of various objects, events, and human nature. It is an order of things remembered and expected as well as things actually perceived, an organized conception of what is plausible and what is possible; it constitutes the matrix through which one perceives his environment (1955: 564).

The sociologist or sociologically oriented social psychologist contends that members of different social units have varying perspectives owing to their sharing in different cultures and having different social experiences and attachments (Shibutani, 1955, and Shapiro and Gliner, 1972). The concept of perspective, however, has received little explicit attention in terms of empirical research. One reason for this is its panoramic nature compared to concepts more commonly used in social psychological research. The latter, such as beliefs and attitudes, are considered to be easier to measure.

According to Arnold Rose, however, the study of subcultures actually revolves around the investigation of the ethnic group's perspective. Rose defines subculture as "the distinctive *meanings and values* held by a subgroup in a society and not by all members of a society" (1967: 731). Research applying the concept of perspective to American Jewry is virtually nil. This reflects the lack of such an approach in social psychology in general for the reason already indicated, and the lack of social psychological theory-oriented research on Jews.

Here we employ this concept, using certain variables as key aspects of the perspective of American Jews. We examine the relationship between Jewish identification and each of these variables. Finally we attempt to show how these variables combine to partially form differing perspectives that are related to differing levels of Jewish identification.

In addition to Jewish identification, we have measures of a few selected factors that are also important in describing the perspectives of our respondents. These factors, Jewish values, marginality, and intellectuality, have traditionally been considered correlates, and even consequences, of Jewish identification. Our approach, however, is to explore their relationships to Jewish identification without positing explicit, a priori hypotheses. Description of being Jewish appears better served by presenting our findings and then offering some social-psychological and historical interpretations. In order to present the associations between Jewish identification and the other variables, to be discussed below, we divided the JI Scale scores ($N = 298$) into three groups: low, middle, and high. Since the scores are somewhat higher for the older respondents than for the younger ones, the percentages in each level differ between the generations (see table 3-3).

Traditional Jewish Values

In his analysis of the American Jewish subculture, Lawrence Fuchs finds that "those things most valued by Jews *as Jews* are: (1) Learning (Torah), (2) Charity (Zedakeh), and for want of a better phrase or word (3) Life's pleasures (non-asceticism)" (1958: 599). (Following the Israeli Hebrew usage we label these values *Torah, Tzedakah,* and *Simhah.*) It is not our contention that these values are basic only to Jewish culture or, among Jews, only to the American experience. They are, however, central to the Jewish value system that has existed for centuries, and they still form the core of that system as it appears in contemporary American Jewish communities. Because of differential involvement in the general American culture, differences on such key factors as occupation and generation, as well as differences in other family and personal experiences, the respondents in this study vary in their adherence to these values. (Social psychologists concerned with attitude theory and measurement have pointed out that attitudes and values constitute clusters of beliefs. In this case we are simply measuring our respondents *adherence* to traditional Jewish values, i.e., their acceptance or *belief* in a cultural value.) We would also expect differences in Jewish identification to account for a significant proportion of this variance.

Each of the three values was indicated by one statement in the questionnaire. Respondents were asked to check whether they strongly agree,

agree, disagree, or strongly disagree. Since the men in this study over-whelmingly concurred with these statements, the important distinction seems to be between those who deeply held these beliefs (as indicated by their strongly agree responses) contrasted to those who held these beliefs to a lesser extent (having checked one of the other three categories).

We measured the adherence to the traditional value of Torah by the statement: "The pursuit of knowledge is a man's obligation even if it interferes with business or pleasure." In the father's generation 23 percent strongly agreed with this statement; in the son's generation 24 percent gave the same response. The Tzedakah statement was: "In order to lead a truly ethical life a person must make an effort to help others, aside from those close to him." Here 51 percent of the fathers strongly agreed, compared to 41 percent of the sons. The statement "Everyone has a duty to enjoy life to its fullest" was used to measure Simhah. In this case 34 percent of the older men and 44 percent of the younger men strongly agreed.

That the value of Torah was less likely to be deeply held than either Tzedakah or Simhah can be attributed to its being more antithetical to the American philosophy than the other two values. One figure in American history whose demeanor and mentality appear in bold contrast to that of many American Jews is President Calvin Coolidge. Coolidge, it might be remembered, said, "The business of America is business." This quote is significant for what it leaves out; the pursuit of knowledge. Coolidge's statement implies an a-intellectualism, the impact of which may be seen on the American Jewish community by the less strongly held adherence to Torah compared to Tzedakah and Simhah.

Despite the increased acculturation of the younger generation as indi-cated by their significantly lower scores on Jewish identification and re-lated Jewish beliefs and attitudes (see chapter 3), there was no significant difference between the generations with respect to adherence to Jewish values. As we have already suggested, while these values may be termed traditionally Jewish, the last two are also a part of the value system of the American culture. Hence, the source of these values for the sons may be more here than in the Jewish subculture in comparison to the fathers.

In order to consider the relationship between Jewish identification and traditional Jewish values, we cross-tabulated (table 7-1) the three levels of JI Scale scores with the two levels ("strongly agree," and other responses) of adherence to Torah, Tzedakah, and Simhah, respectively. The cross-tabulations were, of course, computed separately for fathers and sons.

Torah

Table 7-1 shows that for both older and younger respondents a distinct

Table 7-1
Traditional Jewish Values by Jewish Identification and Generation (Percent)

Traditional Jewish Values	Generation					
	Fathers			Sons		
	JI Scale			JI Scale		
Torah	Low	Middle	High	Low	Middle	High
<SA	91	86	62	79	73	75
SA	9	14	38	21	27	25
Total	100	100	100	100	100	100
	(N=23)	(N=43)	(N=48)	(N=66)	(N=60)	(N=49)

$x^2 = 10.40$ gamma = .58 $x^2 = 0.52$[a] gamma = .07
$p < .01$

97

Tzedakah

<SA	61	63	31	68	65	35
SA	39	37	69	32	35	65
Total	100	100	100	100	100	100
	($N=23$)	($N=43$)	($N=49$)	($N=66$)	($N=60$)	($N=48$)

$x^2 = 11.20$ gamma = .45 $p < .01$ $x^2 = 14.07$ gamma = .40 $p < .001$

Simhah

<SA	74	70	58	51	67	48
SA	26	30	42	49	33	52
Total	100	100	100	100	100	100
	($N=23$)	($N=43$)	($N=48$)	($N=66$)	($N=60$)	($N=48$)

$x^2 = 2.16$[a] gamma = .24 $x^2 = 4.57$[a] gamma = .01

Note: $df = 2$ in all tables.
[a]Not significant.

98

minority *at every level of Jewish identification* strongly agree with the Torah statement. Torah is the only value where this occurs. Furthermore, taking fathers and sons separately, we find that for each level of Jewish identification, Torah receives the smallest proportion of "strongly agree" responses of all three values. In absolute terms as well, the pursuit of knowledge at the expense of other considerations does not appear to be a part of most of our respondents' perspectives. Acceptance of the American cultural position on this value is not, for most, negated by a high level of Jewish identification. There is, however, one difference between the generations that should be pointed out. For fathers the percentage who strongly agree with the Torah statement rises from 9 percent to 14 percent to 38 percent as one goes from low to middle to high levels on the JI Scale (gamma = .58); by contrast, the sons proportion of strongly agree responses stays around 25 percent (gamma = .07). There are two issues here. First, the older group shows a positive association between commitment to Torah and Jewish identification, while the younger respondents do not. Second, in the low and middle levels on the JI scale, the percentage of sons who strongly agree with Torah is higher than the percentage of fathers (21 percent and 27 percent compared to 9 percent and 14 percent).

To return to our main finding, the lack of commitment to Torah among most of our respondents regardless of level of Jewish identification, several considerations are suggested. First, the statement's wording places pursuit of knowledge in opposition to other activities. For many of our respondents this is probably an irrelevant dichotomy, since they either feel that they can pursue knowledge while on the job ("mind-work" occupations) or find the time and resources to pursue both knowledge and business or pleasure. Secondly, since knowledge for knowledge's sake is not a dominant American cultural value, our respondents may see quite correctly that for themselves individually and the members of this society collectively, it is virtually impossible to pursue knowledge at the expense of business. Rather, the pursuit of knowledge is seen either as a consequence of business (research and development) or as a beneficent result of business (the Ford Foundation). The vast majority of our respondents, then, as most Americans, appear to see Torah as out of step with American values.

In regard to the positive association between JI and Torah for the fathers, and particularly the considerably higher percentage of those who strongly agree in the high JI group (38 percent compared to 9 percent for low-scorers and 14 percent for middle-scorers on the JI Scale), the nature of traditional religious practice may shed some light on this finding. We know that the more highly identified fathers are more traditional in their religious practice (chapter 3). Such practice demands that certain times, the Sabbath in particular, be put aside for study, and that *no* work be done. The higher percentage of younger men in the low and middle JI levels who strongly agree with Torah compared with fathers in these JI levels provides some evidence that the sons' positive orientation toward knowledge is not for the most part directly based on their involvement in the Jewish subculture. We will return to this theme when we consider the relationship between Jewish identification and intellectuality.

Tzedakah

The relationship between Jewish identification and the value of Tzedakah, or social responsibility (helping others aside from those close to you), is about the same for the sons and the fathers (table 7-1). In both generations about one-third of those scoring low or middle on the JI scale strongly agree with Tzedakah compared to two-thirds of those high on Jewish identification. That those more identified with Jewish life adhere more closely to the value of social responsibility is not surprising. A central aspect of American Jewish communal life has been philanthropy, traditionally aimed at helping members of the local Jewish community and, in the twentieth century, providing relief to European Jews. The last twenty years or so have also seen significant financial aid to Israel. In addition, Jewish philanthropy has also been directed to helping non-Jews. Philanthropy, then, has been a major factor in communal organization and solidarity, and an important mechanism of Jewish involvement for the individual members of the Jewish community. It would follow, then, that respondents scoring high on Jewish identification would be inclined to strongly agree with the value of helping others. What of the other respondents, however? Are there not other bases from which they might strongly adhere to an ethic of social responsibility—other, non-Jewish bases? For most of our respondents, both fathers and sons, the answer is, apparently not. It appears that Tzedakah is a value deeply embraced in the Jewish culture and that those more strongly identified with Jewish life adhere to the value of helping others more than other Jews.

Simhah

The relationship between Jewish identification and agreement on the value of Simhah, or nonasceticism (enjoying life to its fullest), for the two generations (table 7-1) is less clear than the data on the other two traditional Jewish values. For the fathers a minority at each level of JI strongly agree with Simhah, although there is some increase from low to middle to high. In the sons' case, one-half of those with low and high Jewish identification strongly agree, compared to one-third with middle-level JI scores. A few considerations about our respondents' American experience appear useful here. A key event in the lives of the older men, shared by all Americans in their generation, is the Depression. For many this has been decisive in their orientation toward work and security. Coupled with the achievement value in American society, the Protestant ethic, it is unlikely that nonasceticism derives from their American experience. It is possible that to the extent that Simhah does exist as a value for these older respondents, it has its basis in the Jewish culture; it is a Jewish value. Those with higher Jewish identification, then, would be more inclined to strongly agree with the value of nonasceticism.

A quite different picture appears in the younger generation. For them the American experience has been one of relative affluence. Further, nonasceticism is an increasingly important value in this generation. While our younger respondents may not epitomize the children of the "age of Aquarius" or the "pleasure-seekers," some of the value orientation connoted by these labels has probably affected their perspectives. After all, it is some of their peers who are so labelled. While this analysis may apply to most of those who strongly agree with nonasceticism whatever the level of Jewish identification, another interpretation is also plausible: Those with a low level of Jewish identification, being less immersed in the Jewish culture, are more likely to be involved or directly influenced by the contemporary youth counterculture. The low JI respondents' perspectives, then, are derived in large part from their sharing in this culture, a basic theme of which is nonasceticism. On the other hand, those young men who are high in Jewish identification may value nonasceticism from a different cultural basis, the traditional Jewish value of Simhah. We may have two very different sources for the same value.

The dual influence of American and Jewish values on perspectives can be more directly considered by next examining the issue of marginality.

Marginality

The Jewish people have often been cited as the example par excellence of marginality. For thousands of years they have, to varying degrees at different times, maintained their culture in the midst of alien societies. Their "host" cultures were sometimes welcoming, but were usually at least in part hostile. Park described Jewish marginality in the modern era:

When the walls of the medieval ghetto were torn down and the Jew was permitted to participate in the cultural life of the peoples among whom he lived, there appeared a new type of personality, namely, a cultural hybrid, a man living and sharing intimately in the cultural life and traditions of two distinct peoples; never quite willing to break, even if he were permitted to do so, with his past and his traditions, and not quite accepted, because of racial prejudice, in the new society in which he now sought to find a place. He was a man on the margin of two cultures and two societies, which never completely interpenetrated and fused. The emancipated Jew was, and is, historically and typically the marginal man ([1950: 354] Reprinted with permission of the publisher from Robert Ezra Park, *Race and Culture* [Glencoe, Ill.: The Free Press, 1950]. Copyright © 1950 by The Free Press.)

However, Jewish marginality is not merely an aspect of European history. It exists more or less among contemporary American Jews, including of course our respondents in the St. Paul Jewish community. Sherman, in his analysis of Jewish life in this country, argues: "The Jewish personality is always split because the Jews of the Diaspora always live in two or more cultures" (1961: 125). Other groups seek to cast off their marginality by either becoming the dominant group or by completely assimilating. While these reactions exist within the American Jewish community, Sherman believes that many American Jews "accept their marginality as a normal, indeed, desirable, state of affairs" (1961: 125). Sherman contends that while the general American culture induces a separateness from non-Jews, the Jewish subculture fosters an identification with all Jews. This creates among American Jews needs and interests apart from other Americans.

In this study we relied on fixed responses (again in the form: strongly agree, agree, disagree, strongly disagree) to the statement "Sometimes my Jewish view and the American view differ on important issues" as our indicator of marginality. One might well expect to get a relatively small proportion agreeing with this statement, particularly among our younger, predominantly third-generation American respondents. However, contrary to this expectation, and in accord with Sherman's position, more than one-half (57 percent) of the younger respondents agreed with this statement, indicating their own marginality. In the fathers' generation 68 percent responded similarly.

Marginality and its relation to Jewish identification are, then, still vital issues in the social psychology of American Jews. When a respondent checks "agree" or "strongly agree" (the "yes" row in table 7-2) to the statement "Sometimes my Jewish view and the American view differ on important issues," we are on quite solid ground in arguing that by his own assessment that individual's perspective is characterized by marginality. As previously suggested, Sherman finds such marginality to be common and even desirable among contemporary American Jews. On the other hand, Gordon argues that cultural assimilation or acculturation has increasingly diminished the degree of marginality in this group (1969: 478). While these statements are not mutually exclusive in the logical sense, our data much more support the former position than the latter. The percentage of respondents who in effect answer "yes" to the marginality self-report

Table 7-2
Marginality by Jewish Identification and Generation (Percent)

	Generation					
	Fathers			Sons		
	JI Scale			JI Scale		
Marginality	Low	Middle	High	Low	Middle	High
No	43	31	27	52	50	23
Yes	57	69	73	48	50	77
Total	100	100	100	100	100	100
	(N=23)	(N=42)	(N=48)	(N=64)	(N=60)	(N=47)

$x^2 = 1.95$[a]   gamma = .21

$x^2 = 10.46$ gamma = .34
$p < .01$

Note: For both fathers and sons, $df = 2$.
[a]Not significant.

statement within each level of Jewish identification is about 50 percent or greater (table 7-2). This is true for sons as well as fathers. Even among the younger men who are low on JI, the most "assimilated" category, about one-half (48 percent) agree or strongly agree with the marginality statement. What we do not find, interestingly enough, is very strong evidence for the impact of Jewish identification on marginality. In the fathers' group, for instance, those reporting marginality go from 57 percent among the low JI scorers to 69 percent among those in the middle level, but there is hardly any difference between middle and high levels of JI (69 percent to 73 percent). It is likely that the "Jewish view" is fundamental and pervasive in their perspective: fathers would be more inclined to uniformly incorporate this view as part of their perspective. Most, therefore, would agree that their Jewish view sometimes conflicts with the American view. Such agreement holds for all levels of JI among the older generation. Hence, there is no significant relationship between marginality and the JI Scale. The less identified fathers are probably little more exposed or receptive to non-Jewish ideas than are the more highly identified respondents.

The sons' case presents a slightly different picture, although here again our basic finding of marginality across levels of JI remains. Between the low and middle levels there is virtually no difference, about one-half in each category indicating their own marginality. There is a significant jump between these figures and the 77 percent in the high Jewish identification level who in effect answered "yes" to the marginality statement. Here, then, one could argue for high Jewish identification enhancing or contributing to self-perceptions of marginality. In the case of younger men, high Jewish identification may be much more of a conscious, deliberate involvement than it was or is for their fathers. This may imply that they perceive more differences between their Jewish and American views than do the less identified younger men and that they do, indeed, experience more value conflicts than their less identified peers.

A final note of interest is the generational comparison. Overall the sons are almost as inclined to report their own marginality as are the fathers. As a matter of fact, a little higher percentage of highly identified sons (77 percent) than like fathers (73 percent) report marginality. The difference is in the middle-level JI scorers, where 70 percent of the older men compared to 50 percent of the younger men agree or strongly agree with the statement. In sum, we have evidence, which merits further investigation and consideration, of the enduring importance of marginality as an element of the Jewish perspective. What we do not have is an accounting of the sources of this important and pervasive element in terms of Jewish identification.

Marginality as operationalized in our study is an aspect of our respondents' perspectives that derives directly from their being Jewish. However, another central theme in a consideration of perspective in this group concerns an issue that relates to virtually everyone's thinking: intellectuality. In the Jewish case, however, intellectuality is particularly salient because of its traditional association with Jewish social and cultural life. It is to this issue which we now turn.

Intellectuality

No ethnic group in American society approaches American Jewry in the extent of intellectuality found among its members.[1] This trait has been a characteristic of the Jewish people throughout their history. Van Den Haag cites the "enormous emphasis on learning, intellectuality, articulateness, and argument—even argumentativeness—that is characteristic of Jews" (1969: 20). Howard Sachar, a student of Jewish history, notes that Jews have proliferated "in all fields of intellectual endeavor, the purely humanistic as well as the practical." Furthermore, he contends that "historically, the Jews valued intellect perhaps more than any other people since the ancient Athenians" (1958: 395). Philip Gleason, in an article that analyzes the disparity between Jewish and Catholic intellectuality in America, remarks: "Clearly the most relevant aspect of the Jewish background is the well-known tradition of Jewish intellectualism. The immigrant or immigrant-derived Jewish intellectual is but the American representative of a tradition of learning that reaches back to Biblical times" (1964: 166). Intellectuality was found among immigrant Jewish peddlers and is today discernible among Jews in all types of occupations. We are dealing then with intellectuality as more or less a personal set of attitudes or characteristics that define a cognitive style rather than an occupational category. To measure intellectuality among our respondents, we included in the questionnaire two scales from the *Omnibus Personality Inventory* (Heist and Yonge, 1968). These scales, Thinking Introversion and Complexity, yield scores on basic aspects of intellectuality.

High scorers on the Thinking Introversion Scale

are characterized by a liking for reflective thought and academic activities. They express interests in a broad range of ideas found in a variety of areas, such as literature, art, and philosophy. Their thinking is less dominated by immediate conditions and situations, or by commonly accepted ideas, than that of thinking extroverts (low scorers) (Heist and Yonge 1968: 4).

Forty-three true-false items constituted this scale, making the possible range of scores 0 to 43. The mean score for the younger generation respondents was 24.7 compared to 21.3 for the older group. These scores undoubtedly indicate differences ($t = 4.31$, $p < .001$) in enduring intellectual orientations between the respondents in the two groups, but some of the differences may be more transitory. Many of the younger generation respondents have only recently completed their formal education; others are still in school. Therefore, many of the experiences and events alluded to in the items of the Thinking Introversion Scale have until recently been, or are, a part of their everyday concerns. For purposes of this chapter we have dichotomized the Thinking Introversion (TI) scores based on the overall (N = 294) mean of 23.4. With this procedure 56 percent of the sons are above the mean TI score compared to 34 percent of the fathers.

Heist and Yonge define Complexity as follows:

This measure reflects an experimental and flexible orientation rather than a fixed way of viewing and organizing phenomena. High scorers are tolerant of ambiguities and uncertainties; they are fond of novel situations and ideas. Most persons high on this dimension prefer to deal with complexity, as opposed to simplicity, and very high scorers are disposed to seek out and enjoy diversity and ambiguity (1968: 4).

Another thirty-two true-false items made up the Complexity (C) Scale. Here, the younger men's mean score was 15.9 compared to a mean score of 11.8 for the fathers. This difference was also significant ($t = 6.62$, $p < .001$). When the scores are dichotomized at the overall mean (14.3), 63 percent of the sons and 27 percent of the fathers are in the above average or high category.

Our data, gathered as they are entirely from Jewish respondents, do not allow us to assess whether or not Jews manifest more intellectuality than others with similar social characteristics. What our data do allow us to consider is whether varying degrees of involvement and immersion in the Jewish culture, as indicated by level of Jewish identification, is associated with intellectuality, as represented by high and low scores on the Thinking Introversion (TI) and Complexity (C) scales. The common hypothesis regarding this association would of course be that higher levels of Jewish identification would result in high Thinking Introversion and Complexity. As the data in table 7-3 indicate, our findings do not simply or clearly support this hypothesis. Rather, a number of different findings emerge from our analysis.

Looking first at Thinking Introversion in the older generation, the data do indicate that as level of Jewish identification rises, the proportion of respondents scoring high on TI also increases. However, the sons manifest no such association, there being virtually no difference in the percentage scoring high on TI from one level of Jewish identifcation to another. Comparing fathers and sons within each level, we find almost no difference in the percentage of high TI scorers in the high Jewish identification group (about one-half in both generations). In the other levels of Jewish identification, the percentage of younger men high on TI is much greater than that of

Table 7-3
Dimensions of Intellectuality by Jewish Identification and Generation (Percent)

Dimensions of Intellectuality	Generation					
	Fathers			Sons		
	JI Scale			JI Scale		
	Low	Middle	High	Low	Middle	High
Thinking Introversion						
Low	83	73	51	40	46	46
High	17	27	49	60	54	54
Total	100	100	100	100	100	100
	(N=24)	(N=44)	(N=49)	(N=68)	(N=59)	(N=50)
	$x^2 = 8.97$ gamma = .48 $p < .02$			$x^2 = 0.65$* gamma = -.09		
Complexity						
Low	79	75	67	21	51	44
High	21	25	33	79	49	56
Total	100	100	100	100	100	100
	(N=24)	(N=44)	(N=49)	(N=68)	(N=59)	(N=50)
	$x^2 = 1.33$[a] gamma = .20			$x^2 = 13.71$ gamma = -.36 $p < .01$		

Note: $df = 2$ in all tables.
[a] Not significant.

older men. In sum, Jewish identification is related to the intellectual element of perspective, as measured by the TI Scale, for the older respondents; it is not associated with Thinking Introversion for the younger men in this study. More striking is the wide difference between the generations in the percentage scoring high on TI, particularly among those fathers and sons in the low Jewish identification group.

The data on Jewish identification and Complexity provides a somewhat different picture. For the fathers, the differences in percentages of high C scorers according to level of Jewish identification, while in the same direction as in the TI table, are too small to offer much support to the previous finding. Again the data for the younger respondents gives no support to the hypothesis of a positive association between Jewish identification and intellectuality. In this case, those with a low level of JI have by far the highest percentage scoring high on Complexity (70 percent compared to 49 percent for middle JI and 56 percent for high JI). Furthermore, comparison of older and younger respondents within each level shows even greater differences than in the TI table. Here the differences range from 23 points (high JI level: 56 percent of sons high on Complexity compared to 33 percent of fathers) to 58 points (low JI level: 79 percent of sons compared to 21 percent of fathers). Using Complexity as our measure of intellectuality, then, we do not find this element of perspective to be positively related to Jewish identification even among the older respondents. As a matter of fact, among the younger men those with a low level of Jewish identification were much more likely to score high on Complexity. Again there is a major difference in Complexity scores between the two generations, this time at each level of Jewish identification.

While our findings do not firmly support the generally held hypothesis regarding Jewish identification and intellectuality, an important pattern does emerge from these data: in terms of generational differences, Jewish identification is consistently more positively related to intellectuality for the older generation than for the younger generation. Table 7-4 may help to depict this pattern. While the types of association are different for our two measures of intellectuality, in both cases the association for the older generation is more in a positive direction than the association in the younger group.

Regarding Thinking Introversion ("liking for reflective thought," and "interest in a broad range of ideas") we can assume that this characteristic, as well as Jewish identification, is largely shaped by a person's experiences through young adulthood. An important consideration in analyzing generational differences on this element of perspective is the nature of Jewish social and cultural life, in relation to the broader environment, during young adulthood. In this period for the older generation (roughly around World War II) the Jewish community and subculture where much more

108

Table 7-4
Generational Comparisons of Associations Between JI Scale and Intellectuality Scales

Association Between JI Scale and	Type of Association		
	Negative	*None*	*Positive*
TI		Sons <	Fathers
C	Sons <	Fathers	

pervasive factors in the lives of most young Jewish men. Personal interaction, organizational involvement, and experiences in general existed, to a great extent, within the Jewish community. This community and subculture was a rich and vital source of ideas and provided the organizational contexts for their consideration. On the other hand, relatively few other sources and settings for intellectual involvement were open to young Jewish men at this time.

In sum, the milieu that provided a Jewish identification also fostered the characteristic we have called Thinking Introversion. For the younger generation, the situation is decidedly different. Their experiences are no longer so pervasively within the Jewish community and subculture. Other sources and settings provide exposure to a range of ideas and the opportunity for reflectiveness. Thinking Introversion, then, no longer derives from the same milieu as Jewish identification. The different early-childhood-to young-adult experiences of the two generations of Jewish men in this study are largely due to the fact that the Jewish subculture and the general culture have changed decidedly within the last three decades. On the one hand, issues such as anti-Semitism, Zionism, and religious factionalism, which produced ideological divisions and intellectual stimulation within the Jewish community, do not appear vital to most of the younger generation. On the other hand, the general culture has increasingly provided Jews as well as others with sources and settings that contribute to Thinking Introversion. This is manifest in the increased emphasis on higher education and in the issues dealt with by the mass media.

Our interpretation is that Jewish identification was a positive factor in Thinking Introversion for the fathers and inconsequential for the sons. Turning to Complexity ("flexible orientation," "tolerance of ambiguities and uncertainties") as an aspect of intellectuality, we find that Jewish identification seems unrelated to this measure in the older generation and is inversely related to C for the younger respondents. We have, so to speak, simultaneously moved down a notch, keeping fathers more positive than sons regarding the relationship between Jewish identification and intellectuality. However, we still have to consider JI in reference to the Complexity scale, since we are dealing with two new types of association. Let us reverse order and start with the fact of a low level of Jewish identification, yielding a significantly higher percentage of high Complexity scorers (resulting in an inverse association) in the younger generation. If we take high Complexity to indicate a willingness and an ability to suspend belief, a disinclination to accept any particular set of values or ideas as a given, then we could expect those less involved, attached, and identified with a particular community and culture to have this characteristic. Here this applies to our younger respondents, who are low on Jewish identification.

The question now remains as to why being low on Jewish identification does not result in high Complexity scores for the older generation. As a matter of fact, there is a slight (though nonsignificant) trend in the opposite direction. Being "unfettered" from the given set of values and ideas does not produce, for the fathers, high Complexity as a part of an intellectual orientation. We would argue that such a situation does not *in itself* produce high Complexity for the sons, either. The difference may well be that for the younger generation, low Jewish identification results in a lack of immersion in the communal or subcultural ideas and values *at the same time* as other ideas and values of the larger culture may be considered (see our discussion of the non-Jewish sources and settings resulting in high Thinking Introversion) whereas for the fathers lesser immersion in Jewish values and ideas does not so readily lead to a consideration of other values and ideas. For the older generation neither Jewish nor non-Jewish issues or ideas engender a tolerance of ambiguity. If we see any evidence it is that those fathers who are more immersed in Jewish ideas, i.e., more highly identified, are slightly more inclined to have high Complexity scores. One has to suspend belief or be disinclined to accept an idea *about something*. For the fathers at each level of JI these issues, outside of the Jewish community, may be much less salient than for the sons.

Thus, we conclude that TI and C represent two very different dimensions of intellectuality, and it is the former which represents the traditional concept of intellectuality among Jews and, hence, is positively related to Jewish identification in the older generation. Let us recall that TI refers to an interest in abstractions, dealing with ideas, and a liking for reflectiveness. But C refers to a tolerance of ambiguity or a flexibility of thought, which seems to connote a lack of acceptance of a traditional value system. Obviously, this characterisitc is not consonant with the traditional notion of the association between Jewish identification and intellectuality. The traditional Jewish scholar is a student of the Book and not a student of books. In other words, the traditional relationship between these two es to the "intellectual Jew" not the "Jewish intellectual." (See stinction between "the actively ethnic intellectual" and "the _____ ethnic intellectual" 1969: 483.)

In sum, high Jewish identification may be both encapsulating and thought provoking for the older generation, while low Jewish identification tends to open the way for non-Jewish sources of intellectual stimulation in the younger generation.

Perspective, Generation, and Jewish Identification

In this section we combine the elements previously presented into two basic dimensions of our respondents perspectives:—Jewish outlook and intellectual orientation. We analyze how our respondents stand on each of the two dimensions according to both generation and level of Jewish identification. To do this we assign a tertile rank for each of the Jewish value questions, for the marginality self-report, and for the two intellectuality scales (see Methodological Appendix).

Based on these ranks, we characterize the perspectives of our respondents for each level of Jewish identification as weak, moderate, or strong on Jewish outlook and intellectual orientation (table 7-5). While this attempt to typify the perspectives in three categories is necessarily crude, some important observations can be made. Even with such crude measures which lump different responses together, no two categories, either within or between generations, show the same results. Here then is evidence that belies the stereotype that "Jews are all alike" or "Jews all think the same way." It rather supports the joke that Jews are fond of telling on themselves to the effect that two Jews discussing an issue yields a minimum of three opinions. In sum, Jews do not all think alike about Jewish-related issues nor are they homogeneous regarding cognitive style in general.

In the older generation we find the low identified men characterized by a weak Jewish outlook, as would be expected, and a weak intellectual orientation owing in part to the lack of alternative sources of intellectual content and stimulation. The high identified older-generation respondents are expectedly strong on Jewish outlook and slightly more intellectually oriented (based on ranking in the middle tertile on TI). In the younger generation the low identified are weak on Jewish outlook and strong on intellectual orientation. Here there appears to be an incompatibility between these two dimensions of perspective. In this case it may not be mere apathy but hostility toward much of Jewish life that contributes to this situation. On the other hand, those young men who are high on Jewish identification are moderate on both dimensions. The capacity to harmonize and perhaps even to mutually support Jewish outlook and intellectual orientation does then exist among the most highly identified younger men.

Table 7-5
Perspective (Degree of Jewish Outlook and Intellectual Orientation) by Jewish Identification and Generation

	Generation					
	Fathers Jewish Identification			*Sons* Jewish Identification		
Perspective	*Low*	*Middle*	*High*	*Low*	*Middle*	*High*
Jewish Outlook[a]	Weak	Moderate	Strong	Weak	Weak	Moderate
Intellectual Orientation[b]	Weak	Weak	Moderate	Strong	Moderate	Moderate

[a]Weak = sum of tertile ranks = 4-6
Moderate = sum of tertile ranks = 7-9
Strong = sum of tertile ranks = 10-12
[b]Weak = sum of tertile ranks = 2
Moderate = sum of tertile ranks = 3-4
Strong = sum of tertile ranks = 5-6

Recalling that all of our respondents are from one relatively small, homogeneous Jewish community, the above description clearly indicates that a significant amount of variability in perspective exists among contemporary American Jews. Not only do their perspectives vary in terms of Jewish outlook, but there is distinct variability in what we have termed intellectual orientation. On both of these dimensions, generation and level of Jewish identification appear to shape the perspectives of the men in this study. Whether to deal with the cognitive realm in terms of a general concept such as perspective rather than with more specific value and attitude statements, such as discussed earlier in this chapter, depends of course on the questions and issues that are being addressed. However, in terms of presenting a picture of being Jewish to the members of society at large, including its Jewish members, we believe that the concept of perspective and the information discussed in the context of this idea is both appropriate and important.

Summary

Having completed our analysis of the determinants of Jewish identification, we have turned our attention in this chapter to some of its possible correlates and consequences. To do this, we employ the concept of perspective as a way of talking about our respondents' outlook, the way they "see things." In particular we focus on Jewish values, marginality, and intellectuality as salient dimensions of our respondents' perspectives. In each case we explore their relationships to Jewish identification (having divided the JI Scale scores into low, middle, and high) and generation.

The three traditionally fundamental Jewish values we investigated are Torah, the pursuit of knowledge; Tzedakah, social responsibility; and Simhah, nonasceticism. Despite the sons' lower Jewish identification scores and lower related Jewish beliefs and attitudes scores (chapter 3), there were no significant differences between the generations on the adherence to these Jewish values. Of the three values, Torah was adhered to by the least number of people in both generations, but there was an important generational difference in the correlation coefficient between it and Jewish identification. The fathers showed a positive association between Jewish identification and Torah; the sons did not. This is explained by the effect of religious practice on the more highly identified fathers. On the other hand, the higher percentage of sons than fathers who are less identified but who strongly agree with the Torah statement possibly indicates the non-Jewish sources of this value.

Turning to the Tzedakah statement, we find that in both generations about two-thirds of the highly identified respondents adhere to this value compared to one-third of those with low or middle JI Scale scores. It appears that for these respondents the ethic of social responsibility derives in large measure from the Jewish culture and that those who are more attached to Jewish life strongly agree with the value of helping others more than other Jews.

The third Jewish value, Simhah, did not present as clear a picture as the previous two. A minority of the older generation strongly agreed with the Simhah statement, with a slight increase according to level of Jewish identification. About one-half of the sons in the low and high levels strongly agreed, compared to one-third of those who ranked in the middle level of Jewish identification. While the data do not supply strong evidence, it appears that nonasceticism when it does exist among the older men may likely be based on Jewish values. For the younger men nonasceticism is probably derived from the general youth culture, although young men who are highly identified with Jewish life may adhere to nonasceticism as Simhah, i.e., because it is a Jewish value.

We next turn to marginality as a dimension of perspective. The statement used to indicate this dimension was "Sometimes my Jewish view and the American view differ on important issues." Quite unexpectedly, more than half of the younger respondents agreed with this statement; about two-thirds of the fathers also agreed. Among the younger men the highly identified are more inclined to report their own marginality than are the two less identified groups. In this case there may be a more deliberate involvement in Jewish life among the highly identified young men, resulting in a clear sense of marginality. For the older generation there is less variation by level of Jewish identification.

The final factor we investigated was intellectuality. As a dimension of perspective this concept refers to a personal set of attitudes or characteristics, or aspects of cognitive style. To operationalize this dimension we used two scales from a standard psychological inventory. Thinking Introversion refers basically to a liking for reflective thought and an interest in the world of ideas. Complexity reflects a flexible orientation, a tolerance for cognitive ambiguity. The most common hypothesis regarding Jewish identification and intellectuality would be to assume a positive association. Our data do not support such a simple interpretation. Looking first at Jewish identification and Thinking Introversion, the data do show that among the older respondents, as the level of Jewish identification rises, the proportion who score above the mean on the TI Scale also increases. For the sons, however, there is virtually no difference on TI scores according to the level of Jewish identification.

The data on Complexity are somewhat different. For the older generation, while the positive direction of the association remains, it is too weak to offer much corroboration for the previous finding. Furthermore, in this case, the low identified sons have a significantly higher percentage of high Complexity scores than the other two younger generation groups. One pattern that does emerge from these findings is that Jewish identification is consistently *more* positively related to intellectuality for the older group than for the younger respondents. We conclude our analysis of intellectuality with two observations. First, during the period of the father's adolescence the Jewish community was a much stronger, more pervasive factor in a young Jewish man's development. Hence, we would expect, given the nature of the Jewish community at that time, that an attachment to Jewish life would also bring forth an intellectual orientation. This was supported by our data on Thinking Introversion, which brings us to the second point. It is Thinking Introversion rather than Complexity which represents traditional Jewish intellectuality. The former represents dealing with ideas and reflectiveness, which is inherent in the concept of the Jewish scholar. The latter stands for tolerance of ambiguity, which is one step away from a lack of acceptance of a traditional value system. This, of course, would be anathema to the Jewish scholar.

On the basis of the Jewish value statements and the marginality statement, we constructed a Jewish Outook Index; on the basis of the two intellectuality scales we constructed an Intellectual Orientation Index. These two indices provide us a way of talking about two basic dimensions of our respondents' perspectives. In looking at how our respondents rank on these dimensions according to level of Jewish identification and generation, we find that no two subgroups come out exactly alike. It is obvious, then, that a multitude of perspectives exist within the Jewish community. Further, both Jewish identification and generation appear to be important factors in the shaping of perspective.

In sum, this discussiom of being Jewish attempts to indicate how our respondents "see the world" and also to indicate the variability that exists in the ways in which they see it. This, of course, has implications for their own actions and the actions of others toward them. We will take up this and related issues in the next, concluding chapter.

8   Retrospect and Prospect

A few years ago the following statement appeared in a new Jewish publication:

> The American Jewish community is neither in essence or content a community in structure. It has rejected the basic Jewish ethical and communal traditions as they have evolved from the Prophets on down in exchange for the mess (and it is a mess) of pottage which is the American middle class way of life. Neither is it a community, because community means a group of people which knows itself and knows the realities it is facing and responds to them in a manner relevant to the concerns of its people and the situation it finds itself in. Those rich Jews and their hired bureaucratic hacks who have, with incredible chutzpah, appointed themselves the "leaders" of American Jewry are no more representative of the Jews and their interests than the American establishment is of the American people (*Jewish Liberation Journal*, 1969: 1-2).

How accurate is this statement according to our assessment of the Jewish community?

We can make this assessment in terms of three levels of the American Jewish experience: social relationships, the community, and the wider society. In each of these areas we offer our personal perspective and comments on Jewish life both in terms of the individual's Jewish identity and the nature of the Jewish community.

Jewish Identification and Social Relationships

If the people of the American Jewish community were to ask us what our research suggests is the most important way to build Jewish identification among young people, we would have to reply: No one factor alone makes Jewish youth develop a strong sense of Jewish identification. If the focus of efforts, however, is in building and strengthening large-scale formal organizations like the synagogue or the community center, then Jews could conceivably organize themselves into oblivion by neglecting the dimension of informal interpersonal relationships and activities among family and friends. Sociologists have often cautioned against understanding human behavior in terms of an "Oedipus complex." In this case we suggest that Jews be wary of what one pundit has termed their "edifice complex."

On Friendship

The notion of a "special bond" between people whose only common characteristic is their being Jewish appears again and again in casual conversation among Jews. As upper-middle-class members of American society, many Jews are international travelers on business and/or pleasure trips. Hardly one of these trips passes without the travelers telling about this Jewish couple (fellow travelers) or Jewish merchant (native) whom they met in Paris or in San Juan. Jews will say that they seem "just naturally" to gravitate to other Jews at a party or at any sort of meeting. Regarding more long-term, intimate relationships, the vast majority of Jews indicate that most if not all of their closest friends are also Jewish. This interpersonal attraction, this special bond, appears to hold true for most Jews independent of variations in Jewish identification—so long as there is a modicum of Jewish identification. It is not then a relationship of coreligionists or even of cobelievers. It appears to transcend in some way all of the items on our Jewish Identification Scale. Issues, such as common background, common values and attitudes, explain a lot but not all of what we see as a fellowship of people. Jews from different backgrounds with different values tend, nevertheless, to regard their fellow Jews as brothers and sisters. While we have emphasized socialization within the Jewish community and Jewish family, the notion of a special bond among Jews seems to demand that we go outside this context. After a Jew has met another Jew he has a particular view of that person and he wonders about that person's view of him. However, both partners in this meeting say to themselves: "Well, whatever he thinks of me, at least I know it isn't just because I'm Jewish."

One of the most important aspects of Jewish friendship is the belief that a fellow Jew will relate to you personally rather than stereotypically. This may or may not be the case. We have evidence in sociological studies that minority group members often accept the majority-held stereotype, sometimes more strongly than the majority itself. However, Jews *believe* that they will be responded to personally by other Jews.

Another aspect of friendship among Jews, again based on the outside community, is protecting one's fellow Jews. This feeling may be largely a result of the Nazi holocaust. Whatever its basis, the point is that one whom one must defend may also be seen as one whom one must befriend. While this does not logically follow, it does seem *psycho*-logically to follow.

Finally, it should be noted that while Jewish friendship, like friendship in general, usually takes place among peers, this is not the whole story. We believe that even among those of different generations and genders a special empathy and warmth characterizes relationships between Jews. In sum, we join with many other Jews in saying about Jewish friendship relations: "I'm not exactly sure what it is, but I know it's there." Whatever "it" is, in combination with Jewish formal organizations—both religious and welfare—interpersonal relations form the basis for nothing less than a worldwide Jewish community. Further, it seems to us that such friendship relations in addition to family relations form the human essence of the Jewish community.

On Family

As we have just noted, friendship relations are part of the basis of the life of any people. The other part, and the one that students of Jewish life have considered *the* essence, is of course family relations. Traditionally, Jewish religious and social life has rested in large part upon the family. Certainly our own research indicates the centrality of family life for Jewish identification. Again, however, it appears that with a modicum of Jewish identification, being Jewish has major implications for family life. The cohesiveness of the Jewish family has often been noted. It has been seen on the one hand as the supporting base for achievement and "good" character development; on the other hand, it has been viewed as stifling and oppressive, the source of neuroses and other problems. There is undoubtedly an element of truth in both of these views, and one of the hallmarks of being Jewish in contemporary American society is having to wrestle with these contending forces of Jewish family life. We call this a hallmark because being Jewish virtually implies having and being a part of a Jewish family. This is why the question of intermarriage is a never-ending issue among Jews, scholars and laymen alike. Independent of religious practice in the synagogue are the questions about the nature of family life for the Jew who intermarries. It is here that Jewish life either continues or dies for the intermarried Jew.

The relations between parents and children change in the course of development in the Jewish family as in all families. During the child-rearing years through adolescence it is doubtful that the Jewish family is surpassed in its child-centeredness. "Anything for the children" is a phrase that has been heard since the first generation of American Jews, and it is still heard. The Jewish community, both in terms of formal organizations and friends and relatives, expects and even demands that parents show the utmost care and concern for their children. Their sanctions are hardly ever necessary, however, since the Jewish parent has of course internalized the same values. Indeed, as we have said, being Jewish virtually implies a Jewish family. It is in the family of procreation (where one is the parent) that one has responsibility and autonomy regarding one's identity, which includes being Jewish and having a Jewish family. Being Jewish and having a Jewish family, then, become actualized in the family that one creates. This immediately poses a problem not just of Jewish identity and Jewish family life but of identity and family in general. The problem occurs because the parents are the children in another family (that is their parents' family of procreation). Where is one's identity based? Who is one's family? These common problems are exacerbated in the Jewish community, since identity is here so much imbedded in the family. Further, as we noted, Jewish parents often devote themselves to, and in the process deeply identify with, their children during and after the child-rearing years. This is often a source of continual anxiety and conflict for both parents and children, but it is probably most significant during the period of parent-adolescent relations and parent-young-adult relations.

In adolescence the child who probably has been a "good" boy or girl and quite successful in school overtly responds to agents of identity (significant others) besides his parents. While not substituting another family for his parents, he has other reference groups: peers and formal organizations such as the school. This, of course, is a trying time for adolescents seeking to "find themselves" and parents seeking to make sure that their child "turns out all right." Since both Jewish parents and adolescents have been until this period and still are so involved with one another, the period of adolescence is particularly worrisome. However, in many cases the parent-young-adult period, especially during the initial phases of the child establishing his or her own family of procreation (that is, getting married), is even more difficult. Here the child no longer is a member only of the parent's family but is starting his or her own family and is intimately involved in still a third family, the spouse's. Given the close-knit family and the intense parent-child involvement that characterizes most Jewish families, it is no wonder that some parents see their children's activity (starting a family, being involved with in-laws) as signs of resentment or rebellion. Here again we face the powerful impact of the Jewish family, and to the extent that being Jewish means having a Jewish family, this is not a problem of being Jewish that will soon dissipate itself. This is because having a Jewish family implies both being a son or daughter and a father or mother. Again we are not arguing that this is a uniquely Jewish issue, nor even that it is not an intense issue among other people. The point is that Jewish family relations are a central—perhaps the central—social aspect of being Jewish.

On Work

While for many Jews family and friends constitute the network of relationships, for many others there is a third major sector of social life, the world of work and the concomitant work relationships. It is commonly held that

Jews have "made it" in the economic structure of American society. As a simple generalization this statement is undoubtedly true. However, this does not negate the importance or impact of being Jewish on one's economic life or work relationships. Many of the same comments we made concerning friendship apply to work relationships. This is hardly surprising, since work relationships are often also friendship relationships. For instance, the notion of being perceived in terms of personal qualities (rather than stereotypes) by fellow Jews certainly pertains in work relations. While close working relations do exist between Jews and non-Jews, the empathy and warmth that characterize Jewish friends also more commonly characterize the relationships between Jewish colleagues or coworkers. Paradoxically, this closeness or bond allows for extensive and intensive conflict between work associates as it does among family members. It is as if such relationships are so strong as to allow conflict to continually surface. We often find what appears to be a love-hate relationship between Jewish business partners who have worked together for years and years. It would appear that a combination of family relationships (father-son or brothers) and work relationship (family business or business partnership) would even further stimulate this close yet conflicted relationship between any two Jewish men.

In terms of the relationship of being Jewish to economic success in general, the general view is that Jews are doing very well. The question is, however, would they be doing any better if they were not Jews? It would seem to us that in many instances the answer is undoubtedly "yes." Even in the "liberal" sectors of American society, such as administration of higher education, there is evidence to support this view. It is interesting that when the question of discrimination in employment regarding them personally is posed to many Jewish men, the answer is often something like, "No, not to my knowledge" or "Not that I'm aware of." These answers highlight both the possibility of employment discrimination and its insidious nature. While in general being Jewish does not prevent economic success, the evidence is still that it hurts more than it helps, progressive social change notwithstanding. This takes place from the halls of ivy to the boardrooms of major businesses of the American economy such as finance and heavy industry.

On the other hand, being Jewish within the Jewish community provides one with an economic position within a subeconomy. The Jewish professional or the Jewish merchant has his own clientele, the members of the Jewish community. This is based on friendship and family relationships, a sense of supporting "one of our own" among the Jewish clientele, and, not the least significant, particularly in terms of professional services, a trust in the competence of the Jewish practitioner. Finally, aside from occupations that directly serve the public, there are virtually whole industries that are dominated by Jews and in which Jews often deal with one another. Entertainment, clothing, and retailing are three industries that come immediately to mind. Here it not only "doesn't hurt to be Jewish," but these industries are in many communities dominated by Jews.

In sum, the social relationships that constitute the essence of human activity are in myriad ways affected by one's being Jewish. More particularly, we have commented, in this section, on how being Jewish relates to friendship, family, and work relationships. Undoubtedly the level of Jewish identification affects the salience of being Jewish for these relationships. However, we would argue that with a modicum of Jewish identification, being Jewish is a major factor. This modicum probably rests on perceiving oneself as Jewish and recognizing when one is involved in a Jewish-non-Jewish relationship or in a relationship between Jews. In the case of our study among St. Paul Jews, then, this degree of Jewish identification exists in almost all of our respondents. We would think that even in the 1970s among the "liberated," sophisticated population, which supposedly typifies the American Jewish community, our assessment of St. Paul's Jews applies to the Jews in this society in general. All but that tiny minority who deny their being Jewish will, at least when pressed, avow their Jewish identity and, in terms of social relationships, indicate their recognition of the "peoplehood of Israel" or the family which is their fellow Jews. *Dos pintele Yid,* the spark of Jewish identity, remains in nearly all Jews.

We have commented on the relationship between being Jewish and the central social relationships. While our study assesses the impact of socialization experiences on Jewish identification as a way of addressing the issue of being Jewish, it is clear that the current social structure of the Jewish community is itself important for the maintenance and development of Jewish identity. Hence, we must recognize that the relationship between Jewish identity and Jewish communal structure is a two-way street. Further, we can see that the social structure has its impact on Jewish identity largely through the mechanism of interpersonal relationships (figure 8-1).

If one wants to consider policy implications for strengthening Jewish identity and identification, then the most strategic point in this cycle is that of interpersonal Jewish relationships. What the Jewish community can do is provide the organizational and institutional context for the development and maintenance of these relationships. In succeeding sections we shall offer some suggestions along these lines.

We have also argued that Jewish identity and Jewish social relationships can and often do exist with only a modicum of Jewish identification. However, this minimum level is not a "given," a consequence of some pre-

121

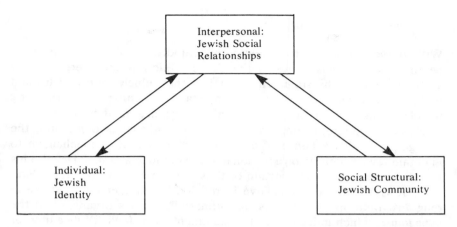

Figure 8-1 Interrelationships Between Individual, Interpersonal, and Social Structural Dimensions of Jewish Identification

or non-social, natural, generic state of being among Jews. As we have seen, Jewish identification is rather a product of social experiences, past and present. More important is the recognition that the just discussed modicum of Jewish identification is dependent on this same experience. The crucial question then is: Does enough of this experience exist to build and maintain a minimum level of Jewish identification? This question must be answered both qualitatively and quantitatively. It is probably true that the proportion of younger Jews who are exposed to and respond positively to Jewish experiences has declined. However, the qualitative question is much more difficult to deal with. It is our view that some aspects of Jewish life within American society offer experiences to which younger people would be positive and receptive. In sum, we believe that the elements of a more viable Jewish community that can provide the requisite experiences for the necessary Jewish identification do exist. We may now turn to a discussion of some of these elements.

The Jewish Community

One of the most famous rabbinic aphorisms admonishes the Jew: "Do not separate yourself from the community." The rabbis were well aware of the importance of being Jewish within the framework of the organized Jewish community and of the consequent effects of the community on the individual.

Synagogue

Without the synagogues most Jews would rapidly assimilate, as appears to be the case for most Jews in the Soviet Union where there are few synagogues. Does this statement mean that other vehicles of Jewish life and indeed Jewish culture are not fundamental? No. Our point is that any people needs some sort of structural or organizational basis for their existence. Aside from being a house of prayer and a house of learning, the synagogue is also a house of congregation. It acts as a mechanism to maintain Jewish identity on a personal, interpersonal, and social level. This is true for the significant portion of those Jews who say something like, "I'm Jewish, but I don't believe in religion." Whether they believe in religious tradition or not, it is the primarily religious organization, the synagogue, which indeed gives the statement "I'm Jewish" meaning, or perpetuates that meaning. We have here an important part-whole paradox: any *individual* can well be Jewish without being a religionist; for *any* individual to be Jewish requires the Jewish religion and its organizational being in one form or the other.

Given this, we must consider the relationship between being Jewish and some of the activities carried out by the synagogue. While synagogue religious services are personally satisfying and fulfilling for some Jews, many, particularly the younger members of the community, find the prayers archaic and irrelevant (whether in Hebrew or English), the history recounted in Bible passages repetitive and uninteresting, and the conduct of the service itself tedious and disjointed. Whether their basic negative response is to *any* religious service or the services found in contemporary synagogues is an important question. For many, we believe it is the former. In this case as well as for those from whom some kind of religious service could be positive, it is important to see Judaism as a code of ethics and the enlightening story of the people rather than as a particular set of *prayers*. However, being Jewish does and must imply a particular set of *practices*, including ritual. Just as we have argued that being Jewish ultimately depends on there being a Jewish religion, there being a Jewish religion depends on people carrying out certain religious practices that distinguish Jews and Jewish life from non-Jews and non-Jewish life. Unitarianism or humanism, then, even if their codes of ethics were exactly the same as that of Judaism, could not result in being Jewish, and being Jewish cannot result in Unitarianism or humanism.

To the extent that the synagogue has captured the organizational basis of Jewish life, in most communities it tends to attract individuals who differ in terms of their Jewish identification. It probably is not that unusual to find a congregation, such as that to which one of the authors belongs, which includes an atheist as well as a Sabbath observant Jew, with many varieties of expression in between, some of which might even include elements of both polar positions. What this implies for the religious activities of the synagogue is that for it to effectively touch the lives of all its members, including many younger ones, *there is a need to provide diversity in the religious programs available.* In terms of religious services this may range from the very traditional to the very innovative: from the formality of the High Holiday services to the informality of five couples meeting in a private home for a Sabbath evening service.

As a final note on the synagogue, we raise the very practical issue of membership dues. Most congregations fix their dues at a particular level, usually too high from the point of view of most congregants. The high rate is due in significant part to the great expense involved in operating the religious school. It is because of this high fee that many younger couples without school-age children do not join the synagogue until their children reach school age. It appears that the synagogue is expecting a major financial outlay before the couple has an idea of what they are "buying." In effect, we have a situation where the synagogue is asking for a commitment before experience rather than providing an experience upon which to base a commitment. Young people should be given the opportunity to experience the synagogue before being asked to carry the normal financial burden. It is our view that *only a nominal sum should be fixed for these couples during their first years of membership or until they have school-age children.* In adopting such a policy, there would be no financial loss incurred by the synagogue, because these persons would not utilize the religious school, which is one of the main drains on the congregation's resources. Indeed, there would be a social gain for the community in building a young couple's commitment from the outset of their marriage.

School

We have already indicated that Jewish education produces a mild but lasting effect on Jewish identification and that this effect is independent of parents and peers. Since adolescence is generally the key stage in the crystallization of identity, the more Jewish education is extended into adolescence, the more effective it will be.

At a conference of Jewish educators attended by one of us, the following exchange was recorded:

Question: If the home is the most important factor in building identity, what can the Hebrew schools do to improve the situation in the home?

Response: Schools must discuss the kind of Jewish identity they are interested in producing and consider alternative models. Parents should be involved in this process.

Question: What if there is "nothing" in the home?

Response: The school indicates to the parents what its curriculum is, not only its texts but its attitudes and commitments as well. The parent is asked if he or she can be comfortable with this, and in what way can the parent contribute to achieving the school's goals. The parent need not subscribe to *all* aspects to be able to make a small contribution (Dashefsky, 1971: 20-21).

Further, *in order to be attractive to adolescents, the curriculum of the Jewish school has to deal in part with issues that the students consider to be crucial in their experience.* Thus, it should include a place for the presentation of a Jewish view on such issues as sexuality, drugs, war and peace, poverty and wealth, etc. Such a program would cultivate a personal philosophy and a code of ethics rather than inculcate dicta and dogma.

Jewish education programs should be a strong and central force in the life of both children and adult members of the American Jewish community. Recognizing that Jews value education for its *extrinsic* as well as its *intrinsic* worth, we must consider Jewish education from a utilitarian perspective. For instance, in this era of rapid transportation, many younger American Jews probably will have the opportunity to visit Israel. A Jewish education program could be geared to the notion that "when you go to Israel, knowing Hebrew will make it a more rewarding experience." Thus, *the learning of the Hebrew language should be made personally useful.*

Also on an extrinsic level, Jewish education should be conceived of as part of one's general intellectual development. There is a need for Jewish education to be recognized as a legitimate element of one's academic credentials. To achieve this, *Jewish education has to be recognized by the wider educational community in terms of academic credit, release time for such studies, and other forms of recognition.*

Turning to the Jewish community, it should *indicate to youth the utility of Jewish education within the Jewish community by making an advanced Jewish education a basis for community leadership positions.* Being a successful physician or businessman does not necessarily qualify one for a position of leadership in the Jewish community.

Moreover, *the school should help define some goals for the parents and their children regarding personal and communal Jewish life (ritual observance, Zionism, etc.).* Parents should be involved in their children's Jewish education. School staffs should explain to them the goals of Jewish education in general and the particular ones they may adopt for their child with appropriate responsibilities for them.

Furthermore, there is a need for *a consolidation of religious schools to create regional Jewish educational centers independent of synagogue control.* Such a measure would free schools of the constraints imposed by the politics, finances, and other pressures of synagogue affairs. Clearly, the synagogues and local Jewish Federation would need to finance such a program. The success of such a program, the Talmud Torah in St. Paul, is highly illuminating.

Lastly, in terms of the community's role in Jewish education, *every child, regardless of his socioeconomic background, should be insured a quality Jewish education.* Some small portion of Jews do not provide their children with a Jewish education or join a synagogue where their children can receive one, because it costs too much. The ability of Jewish education to influence, even mildly, Jewish identification suggests that no human resources be lost or wasted through the financial barriers that may hinder some families.

Finally, although we have no data that explain how much of Jewish identification can be accounted for by the impact of Israel, we do know that Jewish identification and Zionism are highly intercorrelated and that Israel represents an important symbol of that sense of group identification. Moreover, the decision to visit Israel or migrate there generally reflects the individual's Jewish identification. With this in mind, we suggest that *the opportunity for Jewish adolescents to participate in study and travel programs in Israel needs to be expanded.* This experience provides young Jews the chance to observe and to some extent to participate in Jewish life styles different from their own, ranging from the kibbutz experience to the Mea Shearim quarters of Jerusalem's Hasidic communities.

In order for these programmatic changes to be carried out, however, certain structural changes in Jewish community life would have to be made:

All of these efforts take funds. *Here is the greatest challenge facing the Jewish communities: to effectively redistribute the financial resources of the community and its individual organizations, synagogues, welfare, social, philanthropic, and cultural associations, to achieve these goals.* Without a massive restructuring of the priorities and activities of Jewish communities, no effective change will take place. The greater the effort in attempting to carry out planned social change, the more it will permeate the community and the more it will effectively implement the desired change.

Along with this redistribution of resources must come the further democratization of Jewish communal life. The participation in the Jewish community and synagogues of students, teachers, women, professional workers in the community, and nonaffluent Jews needs to be encouraged. The alternative is the perpetuation of an unrepresentative power elite.

It has often been said before that the future of the Jewish community and, therefore, the opportunity to be Jewish depend on Jewish youth. It is for the youth primarily that many of these changes in the synagogue, school, and community are suggested. Indeed, we should look to those communities where such innovations are being implemented as "model communities" to assess their impact on the youth.

The Wider Society

We began this book by arguing that it was not sufficient to focus on the relationships between Jews and other groups in American society. Since we have carried out an investigation of the interpersonal sources of Jewish identification, we must, however briefly, deal with the issue of being Jewish in the wider American society.

Economy

In an analysis of the historical types of constraints operating on Jews within the economic structure in the United States, Simon Kuznets summarized the role of Jewish identification:

> The [Jewish] affiliation constraint, in the case of U.S. Jewry, was reflected in a double reluctance: to work as an employee in a large economic unit, where the rigid rules imposed by the dominant majority would make it difficult for a Jew, if religious, to remain observant, and if secularized, to advance to high levels; and to pursue his occupation in a small-/or even middle-size city where the protective anonymity of the large cities was non-existent, and where clustering with other Jews was restricted by the narrow base for "Jewish" occupations (1972: 11-12).

Nevertheless, American Jews are well integrated into the economy, and they appear to be increasingly well-off. An issue here then is not economic success, but the relationship between being Jewish and such success. It would seem that these two phenomena are becoming more and more disassociated. With a large proportion of professionals and businessmen working within large-scale organizations, being Jewish may be neither a hindrance nor a help. What we do find, owing to the disporportiomate number of Jews in this type of occupational situation, is a high degree of mobility. This mobility is both "vertical" (ascending the occupational hierarchy) and "horizontal" (moving, both organizationally and residentially, from one location to another). While such movement may indicate success within the general economy, it retards integration into the local community's economic and social structure. This situation characterizes many contemporary Americans, non-Jewish as well as Jewish. Paradoxically, the problem of "finding a home" in a community is exacerbated by being increasingly acceptable and accepted in the society at large.

The strong family orientation already noted, in combination with a career orientation that demands geographic mobility, poses a significant problem for many Jewish families. This situation demands that we recall the experiences of our immigrant parents and grandparents who formed mutual aid societies, or *Landsmanschaften,* in order to find security in a strange environment. *The implication here is that local Jewish communities or synagogues consider a new kind of "immigrant" association to provide information and social contacts for the newcomers.* Such groups would facilitate the newcomers' social integration into the community.

Politics

The politics of American Jews are based on an enigmatic mixture of justice, compassion, and self-interest. This takes at least two major forms: mainstream politics, which involves supporting candidates and issues defined as center and slightly left of center, and "New Left" politics, which goes from moderate liberalism to nihilistic radicalism. This distinction helps us understand what happened in the 1972 election among the Jewish electorate. President Nixon received the greatest proportion of Jewish votes in the recent past. His appeal was to "middle America" and the conservation of the American system. The Jewish response to this appeal merits our consideration.

There has been much discussion in recent years, particularly prior to this election, about the supposed increasing conservatism of American Jews. Some have argued that their political orientation has remained relatively constant while there has been a "shift to the left" in American politics. While it is difficult to talk in absolutist terms, it appears, nevertheless, that many Jews have become more conservative. Of the many complex factors that are involved in this issue, one important factor is that many American Jews have become more conservative because they have more to conserve.

On the other hand, many Jews who voted for Nixon did so more in opposition to the candidacy of George McGovern than in support of the incumbent's policy. They had come to define McGovern as too far left of center and associated him with the New Left. This term had become a code word for some Jews for a political stance inimical to Jewish interest, e.g., support of Arab terrorists and certain American anti-Semitic interests.

The previous analysis not withstanding, two-thirds of the Jewish electorate did vote for the Democratic candidate. A fundamental reason for this vote is the longstanding tradition of support for and involvement in the Democratic party. Beyond this, Senator McGovern stood for many of the political ideals Jews espoused. This brings us to a consideration of the traditional liberalism of the Jewish voter.

This is a complex area for analysis, which we can only briefly discuss. Jews have been and continue to be more liberal politically than other groups with similar socioeconomic characteristics. What sustains this liberalism has probably something to do with the experience of being Jewish. Does liberalism derive from such an identity and the litany of persecution and discrimination that has been the Jews' lot from Haman to Hitler? Or does liberalism result from the personal experience of sharing in a Jewish value system with its emphasis on social justice? Probably to some extent both are operating.

It seems to us that that Jews will remain politically liberal to the extent that they see themselves as a minority group in American society which is victimized by the dominant group either politically, economically, socially or culturally. Further, adherence to the ideals of the Jewish humanistic tradition facilitates the liberal orientation. These factors helped to make socialists and Zionists out of many Eastern European Jews. Such people were the primary socialization agents for the contemporary generation. In fact, it is likely that among American Jews the most liberal are direct heirs to these traditions of their grandparents and parents.

Intergroup Relations

The issue of intergroup relations and being Jewish is a double-edged sword. On the one side the blade cuts the Jews as victims of anti-Semitism, and on the other edge the blade cuts the Gentiles as victims of Jewish ethnocentrism.

While God may be dead, as some Christian theologians argued in the 1960s, Christian anti-Semitism is not. It may be resurrected from the gray limbo in which it resides whenever a severe political or economic dislocation in American society occurs. From the firm conviction of friendly Gentile neighbors that Jews are the smartest "race" to employment discrimination in the "executive suite," the specter of anti-Semitism remains.

While American Jews have not been victims of a holocaust, threats elsewhere have caused some trepidation. The vision of another mass loss of Jewish lives indelibly seared the minds of many American Jews during the Six Day War of 1967 and again during the Yom Kippur War of 1973. The action of terrorists who captured and killed members of the 1972 Israeli Olympic team in Munich was a gripping reminder of the Germany that once was. The memory of another Inquisition agitated American Jews to actively demonstrate their solidarity with Soviet Jews through petition, protest, and telephone calls. To the extent that an attack on Jews anywhere is viewed as a threat to Jews everywhere, such an attack will strengthen Jewish identification through the creations of organizational structures and interpersonal relationships.

The prevailing viewpoint in the social science literature is that loyalty to an ingroup tends to be associated with hostility toward the outgroup. If so, can one be highly identified with one's ethnic group and have a low degree of ethnocentrism? While this is not frequently the case, it is possible. The extent to which it occurs depends on the individual's sense of legitimacy and security in his or her ethnicity coupled with a tolerance for differences among peoples. This might be achieved in the Jewish community by emphasizing *the relationship between the particularistic ideals of Judaism and its universal ideals.* Today many American citizens from the ranks of poor people, young people, women, black people, and other oppressed minority peoples are demanding justice. It was the ancient Jewish prophet Amos who first proclaimed: "Let justice well up as waters, and righteousness as a mighty stream." It was the contemporary prophet of his people, Martin Luther King, who reiterated these words. The connection should not be lost by too parochial a view.

The Chain of Generations

At the beginning of this chapter we presented an example of a type of youthful rhetoric that castigated the older American Jewish leadership. While our study shows that significant differences between generations exist in the experience of being and becoming Jewish, it is important to keep in mind that such generational differences existed between the immigrant Jews and their children as well. Indeed, the differences may have been greater and the conflict more strident than that between the committed young critics of contemporary Jewish life and their elders.

The question then arises: Why is it that generational differences appear so intense today? First, the style of conflict is different on the contemporary scene. The crisis in authority in American society has brought conflict between parents and children more into public discussion. Younger people may not be disobeying their parents any more than did their own parents, but people may be more willing to talk about it. Indeed, there may be a kind of "rap gap." Young people may know better how to argue and discuss issues with their parents, who, unaccustomed to such responses, rely on traditional clichés which further alienate their children.

Moreover, the mass media have displayed this conflict more widely than ever possible in previous eras. Consequently, individuals have become more conscious of differences based on generation and more willing to accept explanations on this basis. This is not to obscure the significance of generational differences but rather to place the so-called generation gap in perspective of the rap gap.

Much of American Jewish life mirrors the practices and prejudices of the larger American Society. Despite this tendency, the ethical tradition of Judaism should impel Jews to develop model forms of behavior and organization rather than merely reacting to American society. Thus, though our assessment is that Jews do constitute an organized community, the successful transmission of Jewish identity from generation to generation and the creative survival of the Jewish people will depend on the community's ability to restructure itself.

The rabbis once asked: "Who is the wise one?" Being wise themselves, they answered: "He who sees what is being born."

Conclusion

The comments in this concluding chapter aside, we have tried to present a straightforward account of our study of Jewish identification in a contemporary American community. While recognizing the importance of the intergroup relations level of analysis, we have focused on individual experiences as they relate to becoming Jewish. A quantitative study cannot probe the depths of each persons' experience to show the dynamics of how and why one thinks and behaves the way one does. What it can show is how certain social experiences, common to a number of people, relate to a particular characteristic—in this case, Jewish identification. This we have done. Further, our assessment of the correlates of Jewish identification indicate that we are dealing with a very real and viable issue. In other words, our findings indicate that there are important consequences of being Jewish.

Regarding Jewish identification, both its development and its consequences, we would conclude on the positive note with which we began this book. Becoming Jewish, or, more analytically, the development of Jewish identification, is in large part a function of growing up in a Jewish family and being involved in other Jewish institutions. To the extent that such families and institutions are personally enriching and supporting, individuals will continue to become Jewish. Further, to the extent that being Jewish stands for something particular in terms of personal and group values, principles, and goals, individuals will continue to manifest at least that "modicum" of Jewish identification. It is our belief that the values and goals that underlie Jewish life merit more than this modicum. It is also our belief that the *people* who *are* contemporary Jewish life can make becoming and being Jewish a positive, important part of experience for both themselves and their children.

Methodological Appendix

This presentation of further methodological details beyond those briefly outlined in chapter 2 is divided into several sections. Much of this discussion describes the data-collection procedures utilized in the St. Paul Jewish Study Project (see Dashefsky, 1969 and Shapiro, 1969). An important addition to this is the section dealing with the measurement of variables where we describe the scales and indices used in the present study, many of which were constructed especially for this analysis.

The first section presents a discussion of how the respondents were selected. The second part describes how the data were collected. The third section reviews how the scales and indices utilized in the present study were constructed. Finally, we discuss the techniques used to gather the information on the social history and organization of the Jewish community of St. Paul described in chapter 2.

Selection of the Respondents

The respondents were selected in two categories. The primary group included all young male adults between the ages of twenty-two to twenty-nine inclusive (as of December 31, 1968) residing in metropolitan St. Paul or belonging to a Jewish organization in St. Paul. Ausubel, in gathering data about parent-child interaction, reported:

In this area of investigation retrospective data from young adults are superior to current data from adolescents, since the passage of years permits the individual to evaluate problems otherwise distorted by the influence of current vivid emotion with greater perspective and objectivity (1954:225).

Middleton and Putney examined the relationship between deviation from parental political viewpoints and parent-child relationships (1963). The subjects selected for study included individuals in transition to young adulthood. According to the authors this stage in the life cycle was close enough to the stress of adolescence yet distant enough to recall it with a measure of objectivity.

The proximity of the Twin Cities of St. Paul and Minneapolis made it possible for individuals to reside in the Minneapolis area and belong to a synagogue or Jewish organization in St. Paul. Hence, the dual basis for inclusion of individuals in the population was adopted.

In order to arrive at some estimate of the number of Jewish males in these eight age cohorts, records at the Student Counseling Bureau of the University of Minnesota were consulted. These records included a listing

131

of the religious preference of all students in the senior classes of St. Paul high schools for the past several years. The question may arise as to why the individuals on these lists did not serve as a basis for the selection of subjects. The answer is that data on the religious affiliation of individuals were strictly confidential. Group data were available, but individual names were not released.

Those males who in 1968 were aged twenty-two to twenty-nine would have been in their senior year in high school (or about seventeen) from 1963 back to 1956. Of those eight senior class lists, six were available for examination. A total of 343 males, or a mean of 57 in each class, declared themselves to be Jews. Over the eight-year period this would raise the total number of avowed Jews to 457. This estimate of the number of Jews in St. Paul aged twenty-two to twenty-nine was subject to two biases. First, not all high-school seniors commonly identified as Jews would necessarily declare themselves to be Jews. About 80 more students probably did not declare themselves as Jews, bringing the total to 537. The figure 80 was suggested by the results of the examination of the surnames of all male seniors. For the six lists examined there was a mean of ten students per year who had apparently Jewish surnames, but listed no religion. It should be pointed out that St. Paul has a large number of persons of German origin, whose surnames may be confused with Jewish ones. Thus, the figure of 537 probably was the upper limit for this estimate.

The second bias to which this estimate was subject involved the substantial gap of five to twelve years between the time these individuals were in high school and the time they were to be included in the study. This population faced great attrition in numbers due to the following considerations: (1) Some young men were studying out of town. (2) Some were away in the armed services. (3) Others had moved out of St. Paul to Minneapolis or its suburbs and had affiliated with community associations there. (4) Finally, some young men had migrated to other parts of the country to seek new employment opportunities. As the community analysis indicated, a sizable portion of St. Paul's young Jewish men did not remain in their native city.[1] It was conservatively thought that the number of individuals in the eight original cohorts would be reduced by perhaps 25 to 50 percent, leaving roughly 275 to 400 men in this age group.

The actual listing of the members of the population was constructed by examining available lists of synagogues and other organizations. Members of the community cooperated by checking and adding names to these lists. Each synagogue was approached and cooperated in drawing up a list of young men, aged twenty-two to twenty-nine (and their fathers), who either were members of the congregation or were sons of members. The overwhelming majority of names on the list came from the two largest synagogues, the Conservative and the Reform temples. Of the younger respondents, 18 percent were not synagogue members. In addition, the young men's list of the United Jewish Fund and Council and the religious census of Jewish graduate students on file at the Hillel House were consulted for additional names. In sum, a total of 321 "sons" aged twenty-two to twenty-nine was included in the listing, a total within the estimated range of 275 to 400.

The second group of subjects included the fathers of sons aged twenty-two to twenty-nine. Many of the fathers' names were obtained through consultation with community members. This listing of fathers was much shorter than that for sons because some fathers were deceased, some were living out of town, and some had two or more sons included in the population. Only 3 percent of the older generation respondents were not synagogue members. This percentage does not appear to indicate a significant bias since a very high percentage of men in this generation (well over 90 percent) are synagogue members. A total of 214 fathers was included in the final listing.

The lists of sons and fathers totaling 535 individuals represented populations—not samples—including nearly all Jewish men aged twenty-two to twenty-nine living in St. Paul or belonging to a Jewish organization in St. Paul and their fathers who were alive and living in the metropolitan area. We, therefore, made the assumption that our respondents constitute a sample of a hypothetical population of Jewish men in this age range in American Jewish communities of similar size (Hagood and Price, 1952: 293). Hence, statistical tests used permit inferences about this hypothetical population. The study population was biased towards affiliation with Jewish associations. An attempt was made, however, to reach some small but unknown number of sons and fathers who were neither identified with a synagogue or Jewish organization, through publicizing the project in the local press. Only one father and his son were added to the list on this basis. Nevertheless, it should be reiterated that the listing of sons included 18 percent who did not belong to a synagogue, while the listing of fathers included 3 percent.

Data Collection

The data utilized in this study were gathered in the St. Paul Jewish Study Project. The questionnaire was initially utilized in a pilot study, and some modifications were introduced.

Procedures in Mailing Questionnaires

Since 535 persons were to be contacted and the pilot project had indicated no significant advantage to personal delivery, it was decided to mail out the questionnaire. Observing some of the suggestions offered by Parten (1950: 383-402) with regard to mail procedures, the questionnaires were mailed out during the first week in March 1969, so as to arrive prior to the weekend. The questionnaire was accompanied by a cover letter explaining the purpose of the research and assuring the individual that his name would not be associated with any information that would be released publicly. The letter included a list of community leaders who had agreed to act as sponsors of the project, providing assurance of its credibility.

A letter reminding individuals who had not responded to the questionnaire to do so was sent out two weeks later. Another questionnaire with a new cover letter was distributed the following week to those who had not yet responded. Finally, another letter was sent out one week later to those who still had not responded. This letter included a handwritten postscript stating that the individual's cooperation would be deeply appreciated.

Prior to and during this period of successive mailings of the questionnaire, articles dealing with the research project appeared in the local daily newspapers, the neighborhood and Anglo-Jewish weeklies, and the weekly bulletin of the largest synagogue. All publicized the study and encouraged individuals to fill out their questionnaires.

Response Rate

In the population of younger men, 183 questionnaires were returned, representing 64 percent of the total of 286. This total represented a little more than half of the total of 537 who were seniors in St. Paul high schools in 1956-63. The prevalent assumption that young Jewish men were not remaining in St. Paul was supported by this finding. This figure of 286 revised from the original one of 321 was also within the estimated range of Jewish men in this age cohort. For the population of older men, 119 questionnaires were returned, representing 63 percent of the total of 191. In sum, 302 usable questionnaires were returned, constituting 63 percent of the revised total number of cases of 477. This revision of the total number of cases from 535 to 477 is due to the fact that a total of 58 sons and fathers who received questionnaires were eliminated from the study because they were improperly identified as belonging to the population. In some cases the persons were no longer living in St. Paul or were too old, or not alive. It is probable that some portion of the non-respondents also did not fit the population, but it is not possible to ascertain how many. This figure reflects the response rate for all actual population members to whom the questionnaire was sent. Undoubtedly some of the men on our lists did not receive the questionnaire for one reason or another. Hence, our response rate for those actually contacted is somewhat higher than the figure reported.

Among the returns there were 98 pairs of a son and his father. In nine cases two sons (brothers) returned their questionnaires, and both of them were paired with their father. Since 187 cases (65 percent) represented sons and their fathers, the amount of difference was reduced because they shared certain similar family experiences and characteristics. Consequently, within the groups of sons and fathers these individuals more accurately reflected differences due to generational influence.

For both groups of sons and fathers, the majority of returned questionnaires arrived in response to the first mailing: 54 percent and 53 percent, respectively. The reminder brought in 17 percent more of the total number of sons and 13 percent of the fathers. The second mailing of the questionnaire brought in 13 percent more sons and 15 percent more fathers. The subsequent personalized reminder was the most effective follow-up, bringing in 17 percent of the sons and 19 percent of the fathers. There was no significant difference in the response rate for sons and fathers for the four waves of returned questionnaires.

Nonrespondents

In order to establish whether there were any significant differences between the respondents and the nonrespondents, a comparison was made on the basis of three relatively easily obtainable pieces of information: occupation, synagogue membership, and residence. The occupations of the nonrespondents were obtained by consulting the city directories for St. Paul, Minneapolis, and their suburbs. The information on membership and residence was derived from the synagogue listings.

There was no significant difference between respondents and nonrespondents among occupations for the younger men. There was, however, a significant difference for the older men among occupations of respondents and nonrespondents. (Chi square = 43.7, $p < .001$, $df = 6$, $C = .45$.) Nonrespondent fathers tended to have higher-level occupations than respondents. This difference can be explained by the imperfect listings of occupations in the city directories. In many cases only the name of the business or firm was listed with no occupational title. In the absence of this latter piece of information, the inference was then made that the individual owned the business and this tended to increase the number of high-ranking occupations. Among the sons this did not pose a problem, because fewer of them owned or were employed by local businesses. In addition, a substantial number were listed as students, a clearly discernible category.

There was no significant difference for fathers between respondents and nonrespondents with respect to synagogue affiliation. There was, however, a significant difference for sons in this regard. (Chi square = 66.7,

$p < .001$, $df = 3$, $C = .44$). Nonrespondent sons appeared more likely to be nonmembers than respondents. This difference can be explained by the imperfections in the data gathered for the nonrespondents. Many of the sons reported that they were synagogue members even though their names did not appear on the official lists because the membership was in their fathers' name.

With regard to residence there was no significant difference for fathers between respondents and nonrespondents. For sons, however, there was a barely significant difference between respondents and nonrespondents with respect to residence. (Chi square $= 4.76$, $p < .05$, $df = 1$, $C = .13$.) Nonrespondent sons were somewhat more likely to live in Highland Park. A good number of nonrespondents were probably out of town at school or in the armed services but still had their permanent address with their parents. This would corroborate the previous significant difference regarding synagogue membership. Thus, it seems that the biases reported are more likely to reflect the difficulties in collecting accurate information on the nonrespondents rather than any systematic difference between them and the respondents.

Measurement of Variables

JI Scale

As we indicated in chapter 2, there were thirty-one items in our questionnaire that measured various beliefs and attitudes toward specific and general areas of Jewish life. Each of these items was measured in terms of a four-point Likert scale measuring the extent of the individual's agreement with each statement (strongly agree, agree, disagree, strongly disagree). Through the technique of factor analysis we were able to reduce the number of items to the seven most highly intercorrelated ones that yielded a one-factor solution. The factor was subsequently identified as representing the dimension of Jewish group identification.

Table A-1 presents each of the seven items included in the one-factor solution. The first column indicates the factor loadings on which basis the items were selected for inclusion. The second column presents the communalities which represent the squared value of the corresponding factor loadings. The construction of the composite factor scale for each observed case in our data-set utilizes the factor-score coefficient in column three. This coefficient is multiplied by the corresponding standardized score (Z) of the variable for each respondent, where $Z_1 = $ (variable 1 $-$ mean of variable 1)/standard deviation of variable 1. This product is computed for

Table A-1

Factor Loadings, Communalities, and Factor Score Coefficients for Variables in JI Scale (Based on Principal Factor Without Iteration Method)

Variable	Item	Factor Loading	Communality	Factor-Score Coefficient
1	I feel an attachment to the local Jewish Community	.740	.547	.204
2	I feel an attachment to American Jewry	.742	.551	.205
3	Of all foreign countries, I feel the strongest ties to Israel	.657	.431	.181
4	I feel a strong attachment to Jewish life	.850	.723	.235
5	My general outlook has been affected by my sharing in the Jewish culture	.678	.459	.187
6	[I] think it is important to know the fundamentals of Judaism	.639	.408	.176
7	[I] feel a close kinship to Jewish people throughout the world	.709	.503	.196

Note: Responses were scored strongly agree = 4, agree = 3, disagree = 2, strongly disagree = 1.

each of the seven variables, and subsequently the products for each variable are added together. The resulting sum represents the respondent's factor-scale score on the Jewish Identification (JI) Scale. (For further details on computational procedures see Nie, Bent, and Hull, 1970; especially 226ff). The construction of the factor scale in this way yields a mean scale score of 0 and a standard deviation of 1 (see table A-3).

While these seven items loaded highest on the first factor, they loaded on other factors as well, indicating that there may be other components and dimensions to Jewish identification. This observation has been reported in previous efforts to measure Jewish identification (see Segalman's review article, 1967). Nevertheless, in our analysis the factor structure was too unstable to permit subfactoring, and the one-factor solution with a loading cutoff point of .64 was accepted. As we indicated in chapter 3, our factor solution seemed to support the notion of the centrality of Jewish peoplehood in the study of Jewish identification.

Such a scale based on factor analysis has a built-in measure of reliability in the form of the internal consistency of the items utilized being measured by the factor loadings. (For a discussion of validity see chapter 3).

Jewish Beliefs and Attitudes

The other twenty-four items about Jewish life which were not utilized in the seven-item factor scale of Jewish identification provided the bases for the construction of several related indices of Jewish beliefs and attitudes. A correlation matrix of these items indicated that at least three other dimensions existed: Zionism, Orthodoxy, and Christmas observance.

Table A-2 presents the intra-index item correlations for these three variables. Zionism was conceptualized as more than merely supporting Israel, which applies to most American Jews. Indeed, one of the items *not* used was "[I] think Israel should be supported." The items in the Zionism Index indicate the individual's concern with the centrality of Israel in Jewish life. Such a concern ranged from a desire to visit Israel above all foreign countries to a consideration of living in Israel. The five items of the Zionism Index had a mean correlation of .41.

Orthodoxy was conceptualized in terms of the notion of Torah—true Judaism supported by Orthodox Jews, i.e., a belief in divine revelation and the consequential centrality of observance of the 613 *mitzvot*, or commandments, summarized in the Torah and other sacred Jewish books. It is important to note that our Index of Religious Orthodoxy applies to belief and not behavior. The two items of this index had a correlation coefficient of .46.

Christmas observance was employed as a measure of the extent of

Table A-2

Intra-Index Item Correlations (r) for Zionism, Orthodoxy, and Christmas Observance

Zionism	1	2	3	4	5
1. If I were to learn another language, I would most like to learn Hebrew (assuming I did not know it)	—	.40	.36	.56	.40
2. [I] consider (or considered) living in Israel		—	.23	.49	.19
3. [I] think it is important that Israel remain a "Jewish State"			—	.54	.50
4. [I] feel a strong desire to visit Israel before visiting other countries				—	.46
5. [I] feel that Israel is the spiritual homeland of the Jewish people					—

Mean correlation = .41

Orthodoxy	1	2
1. [I] think there are many books more important than the Bible	—	.46
2. [I] feel the Torah is the revealed word of God		—

Christmas Observance	1	2
1. It's all right for Jews to exchange gifts at Christmas	—	.64
2. There is nothing wrong with Jews celebrating Christmas		—

Note: Responses were scored: strongly agree = 4, agree = 3, disagree = 2, strongly disagree = 1, except for the Christmas Observance items, which were scored in reverse order.

identification with the dominant group. The two items of the Index of Christmas Observance had a correlation coefficient of .64.

Table A-3 presents the means and standard deviations for the JI Scale and the indices for Jewish beliefs and attitudes reported in chapter 3. These data are presented for all cases and separately for sons and fathers.

Socialization Variables

There were two key measures developed in this study for our measurement of socialization experiences. The first of these was the Index of Jewish Expectations, which consisted of the summated scores of the degree of perceived expectation for participation in Jewish activities during adolescence. This perceived expectation was based on the response to the question "How would you rate this person's expectations for you to participate in Jewish activities?" It was scored as follows: (−2) very weak, (−1) weak, (+1) strong, and (+2) very strong. This score was computed separately for each of three significant others listed by the respondent in response to the question, "Who was the individual that you knew personally who *most* influenced your thinking? (e.g., brother, friend, teacher)." A weight of 6, 3, or 2 was attached to each of the three significant others according to their being listed first, second, or third. In this way, for each significant other listed, be it father or mother, teacher or friend, a specific measure of perceived expectation could be constructed by multiplying the weight (6, 3 or 2) times the expectation score (−2, −1, +1, +2). In fact, the Index of Jewish Expectations was computed for the influence of these four categories. The perceived expectation scores for each significant other category (i.e., father, mother, teacher, and friend) ranged from a low of −12 to a high of +12. In addition, a score for the combined perceived expectation of family members was also computed. These scores actually ranged from −18 to +18 (although theoretically the scores could have ranged from −22 to +22).

The second socialization measure developed was the Index of Jewish Activities. It consisted of a summated score based on the number of activities checked by the respondent as those in which he participated during adolescence. For each activity the respondent indicated where applicable with whom he participated in this activity. In this way a summated score was constructed separately for parents and friends. The scores ranged from 0 to a high of 14. Following is the checklist of thirty items of Jewish activity:

1. Celebrated Passover Seder
2. Had Sabbath meal on Friday night

Table A-3

Means and Standard Deviations for JI Scale and Some Jewish Beliefs and Attitudes for All Cases and by Generation

Generation									
	Sons			Fathers			All Cases		
Jewish Beliefs and Attitudes	Mean	SD	Cases	Mean	SD	Cases	Mean	SD	Cases
JI Scale (factor score)		1.0	179	0.23	0.90	119	0.0	1.0	298
Zionism	12.7	3.2	180	14.5	2.5	119	13.4	3.0	299
Ingroup Marriage	3.0	0.89	181	3.4	0.62	119	3.2	0.83	300
Christmas Observance	6.3	1.6	183	6.3	1.3	119	6.3	1.5	302
Orthodoxy	4.6	1.4	179	5.7	1.3	119	5.0	1.5	298

3. Attended services on High Holidays
4. Attended services on Sabbath
5. Attended services on other occasions
6. Discussed topics with Jewish themes
7. Spoke Yiddish (at times)
8. Spoke Hebrew (at times)
9. Studied Hebrew
10. Studied Yiddish
11. Studied Jewish sacred texts
12. Studied Jewish history
13. Studied Jewish customs and ceremonies
14. Sang Jewish songs (for pleasure)
15. Lit Hanuka candles
16. Danced Israeli dances
17. Participated in leading youth services
18. Visited in Israel
19. Studied in Israel
20. Attended Jewish camp
21. Belonged to a Jewish organization
22. Kept Kosher
23. Observed the Sabbath
24. Ate only special Passover food on Passover
25. Read Jewish books
26. Read Jewish magazines
27. Listened to Jewish music
28. Read Jewish newspapers
29. Fasted on Yom Kippur
30. Put on Tfillin

Table A-4 presents the means and standard deviations for each of the socialization or structural variables referred to in the text. These data are presented separately for sons and fathers.

Socioeconomic Status

The standardized measure of socioeconomic status utilized was the Two-Factor Index of Social Position. The two factors included in the index are occupation and education.

Table A-4

Means and Standard Deviations for Independent Variables by Generation

	Generation					
	Sons			Fathers		
Independent Variables	*Mean*	*SD*	*Cases*	*Mean*	*SD*	*Cases*
Socialization Variables						
Index of Jewish Expectations,						
Father	1.2	4.7	179	2.3	4.2	119
Mother	1.4	3.7	179	2.1	3.9	119
Friend	1.0	3.4	173	0.05	3.2	119
Family	2.4	6.9	173	4.6	6.7	107
Index of Jewish Activities,						
Parents	2.6	2.0	179	4.6	3.3	114
Friends	2.7	2.9	179	1.3	2.0	107
Older Brother	1.4	0.4	173	1.5	0.50	111
Father's Religiosity	8.0	3.6	173	11.7	5.1	114
Jewish Education	12.3	6.1	173	11.6	6.9	114
Knowledge of Perspective	—	—	—	3.3	0.63	107
Perceived Similarity of Perspective	—	—	—	2.8	0.84	107
Structural Variables						
Jewish Area	0.5	0.5	179	0.77	0.42	117
Proportion of Neighbors Jewish	2.4	0.9	179	2.5	0.77	117
Occupation	2.0	1.0	175	3.9	1.9	109
Education	5.9	1.0	175	4.9	1.4	109
Income	1.8	0.4	169	5.7	1.4	109
Synagogue Attendance	2.5	0.7	169	2.9	0.71	107
Synagogue Membership	2.5	0.8	169	2.7	0.56	117

Occupation is presumed to reflect the skill and power individuals possess as they perform the many maintenance functions in the society. Education is believed to reflect not only knowledge, but also cultural tastes. The proper combination of these factors by use of statistical techniques enable [sic] a researcher to determine within approximate limits the social position an individual occupies in the status structure of our society (Hollingshead, 1957:2).

Both occupation and education were ranked on a seven-point scale: 1 being the highest and 7 lowest. (Students were coded in a separate category and their father's occupation used in computing the index score.) Occupations are coded according to the following categories:

1. Higher Executives, Proprietors of Large Concerns, and Major Professionals;
2. Business Managers, Proprietors of Medium Sized Businesses, and Lesser Professionals;
3. Administrative Personnel, Small Independent Businesses, and Minor Professionals;
4. Clerical and Sales Workers, Technicians, and Owners of Little Businesses;
5. Skilled Manual Employees;
6. Machine Operators and Semi-skilled Employees;
7. Unskilled Employees.

Education was coded according to the categories listed below based on the highest level completed. Given the relatively high levels of education achieved by Jews, the highest category was broken up into two levels (0 and 1):

0. Ph.D., M.D., D.D.S., D.Ed., L.L.B.
1. Master's degree;
2. Four-year college degree;
3. 1-3 years of college;
4. High school or equivalent;
5. Grades 10 or 11;
6. Grades 7-9;
7. Less than grade 7.

Following Hollingshead's procedure, occupation was given a weight of 7 and education a weight of 4. The actual scores for each factor were multiplied by these weights and summed for each indidvidual. Each individual was then categorized into one of five social strata on the basis of his summative score, which could range from 11 to 77. Social class was determined by grouping the index scores as follows:

Class	Score
I	11-17
II	18-27
III	28-43
IV	44-60
V	61-77

Subsequent analysis indicated that the variables occupation and education provided more meaningful results when used separately.

Intellectuality

Two scales from the *Omnibus Personality Inventory* (Heist and Yonge, 1968) were used in this study to measure intellectuality. Both the TI Scale of forty-three items and the C Scale of thirty-two items were described in chapter 7. Each of the items in this inventory required simply a true or false response depending upon whether the respondent felt that the particular statement was true for him or false for him. Since this inventory was usually administered to college students, the following statement appeared in the questionnaire along with the other instructions: "Note—in some questions you are required to answer *as if you were a student*."[2]

Of the numerous cross-tabulations made to ascertain the social background characteristics of high and low scorers on TI, two merit reporting. There were positive although weak associations with occupational rank and education (gamma = .18 and .25, respectively). None of the cross-tabulations between social background variables and C produced a statistically significant association. This includes occupational rank and educational rank (gamma = .01 and .11, respectively).

For 7283 college freshmen (3450 men and 3743 women) at thirty-seven institutions, the mean score on the Thinking Introversion Scale was 25.3 with a standard deviation of 7.9. On the Complexity Scale the mean score for these students was 15.3 with a standard deviation of 5.5 (Heist and Yonge, 1968:11).

For the younger generation respondents the actual range of scores on the Thinking Introversion Scale was 8 to 39, with a mean of 24.7 and a standard deviation of 6.6. The approximate quartile breakdown was as follows: 24 percent (44) had scores of 8 to 19; 25 percent (46) had scores of 20 to 24; 26 percent (47) had scores of 25 to 29; and 24 percent (44) had scores of 30 to 39. There were two nonrespondents to the Thinking Introversion Scale.

On the Complexity Scale the range of scores for the sons was 4 to 30, with a mean of 15.8 and a standard deviation of 5.5. The distribution collapsed into the following quartiles: 24 percent (44) had scores of 4 to 11; 23 percent (41) had scores of 12 to 15; 28 percent (51) had scores of 16 to 20; and 25 percent (45) had scores of 21 to 30. There were two nonrespondents to the Complexity Scale.

The range of scores on the Thinking Introversion Scale for the fathers was 6 to 40, with a mean of 21.3 and a standard deviation of 6.9. These scores were divided into the following approximate quartiles: 21 percent (25) had scores of 6 to 16; 28 percent (33) had scores of 17 to 20; 25 percent (29) had scores of 21 to 25; 26 percent (30) had scores of 26 to 40. There were two nonrespondents to the Thinking Introversion Scale.

The fathers' scores on the Complexity Scale ranged from 2 to 27, with a mean of 11.8 and a standard deviation of 5.1. These scores fell into the following quartiles: 27 percent (31) had scores of 2 to 8; 21 percent (25) had scores of 9 or 10; 25 percent (29) had scores of 11 to 14; 28 percent (32) had scores of 15 to 27. There were two nonrespondents to the Complexity Scale.

Perspective

Table 7-5 (Perspective by Jewish Identification and Generation) is derived from table A-5. For each category based on generation and JI level (e.g., fathers with middle JI Scale scores) a rank was determined for each variable in the table. In the cases of Torah, Tzedakah, and Simhah the rank was determined in the following way: Rank 1 was given if 33 percent or less of the respondents in that category *strongly agreed* with the statement used to measure the variable in question. Rank 2 was given if between 34 and 67 percent strongly agreed. Rank 3 applied if more than 67 percent strongly agreed. For marginality, the rank was determined by the percentage who *strongly agreed or agreed* with the marginality self-report item, according to the same system used for the Jewish value statements. For the TI and C scales the rank was determined by the percentage who scored above the mean on these intellectuality scales again with rank 1 assigned if 33 percent or less scored above the mean, rank 2 assigned if between 34 and 67 percent scored above the mean, and rank 3 assigned if more than 67 percent scored above the mean.

Data Sources for Community Research

Information on the St. Paul Jewish community was gathered in part through

Table A-5
Ranks* (1, 2, or 3) Based on Percentage Adhering to Elements of Perspective by Jewish Identification and Generation [a]

Elements of Perspective	Fathers JI Scale			Sons JI Scale		
	Low	Middle	High	Low	Middle	High
Jewish Outlook:						
Torah	1	1	2	1	1	1
Tzedakah	2	2	3	1	2	2
Simhah	1	1	2	2	1	2
Marginality	2	3	3	2	2	2
Intellectual Orientation:						
TI	1	1	2	2	2	2
C	1		1	3	2	2

[a]Ranks are based on the following percentages: 1 = ≤ 33 percent; 2 = 34-67 percent; 3 = > 67 percent. The exact percentages for Torah, Tzedakah, and Simhah may be found in table 7-1, for marginality in table 7-2; for TI and C in table 7-3.

a series of unstructured interviews with nearly all of the rabbis and professional leaders of the major synagogues and organizations as well as members of the community. Seventeen individuals were interviewed during the
middle and late fall of 1968 in sessions ranging from one-half hour to several
hours over two-or three-day periods. In addition to this primary source of
data, several secondary sources were explored. Both the Anglo-Jewish
press and the local St. Paul papers were examined for possible relevant
materials as far back as 1912 in the former case. Particularly useful were
several issues of the *American Jewish World,* a Twin-Cities Anglo-Jewish
Weekly, published on the major anniversary dates of the paper's founding
in 1912. Moreover, numerous other materials including records and docu-
ments of various synagogues and organizations were examined. Finally,
some previously published materials, much of it by local residents, were
reviewed. The Minnesota Historical Society and the American Jewish
Archives were very helpful in providing such materials. This phase of the
community research was conducted prior to the survey research. This
sequence sensitized us to the nature of the community and undoubtedly
made the task of carrying out our survey more efficient in more ways than
we may know (Sieber, 1973).

Notes

Notes to Chapter 2
The Jewish Community of St. Paul

1. This section is adapted from chapter 2 of *The Jewish Community of Saint Paul* (Dashefsky and Shapiro, 1971). See Methodological Appendix for a description of data sources.

2. Much of the review of the early Jewish community's history is based on the work of W. Gunther Plaut (1959), former rabbi of the Mt. Zion Temple.

3. This section is adapted from chapter 3 of the Jewish Community of Saint Paul (Dashefsky and Shapiro, 1971). See Methodological Appendix for a description of data sources.

4. These figures were supplied by the United Jewish Fund and Council of St. Paul.

5. Source: *American Jewish Yearbook;* vol. 1 (1900).

6. These figures were made available by the Jewish Community Center of St. Paul.

Notes to Chapter 3
Methods and Measures

1. This section is a revised version of material first presented in *The Jewish Community of Saint Paul* (Dashefsky and Shapiro, 1971: 25-27, 40). While the data were gathered in one community for one ethnic group, the value of this study is not diminished. As Goldstein and Goldscheider have noted (1968: 233-34), the emphasis needs to be placed on the pattern of relationships among the variables examined and not on absolute statistical values. In the absence of data on American Jewry at large or on ethnic groups in general, studies based on more limited samples yield valuable findings that need to be compared to other studies.

2. Occupational levels were measured according to the technique described in "Two Factor Index of Social Position" (Hollingshead, 1957). See Methodological Appendix.

3. It should be noted that the phrasing of this statement had no specific referent, i.e., "you" or "your child" and that the item was phrased in positive terms with respect to ingroup marriage. A differently phrased question on intermarriage in a study of Boston Jewry (Axelrod, et al., 1962) found much smaller differences between the second and third generations.

150

Notes to Chapter 5
Adolescent Experience and Adult Activity

1. We used the stepwise regression program in the *Statistical Package for the Social Sciences* (Nie, Bent, and Hull, 1970). Graves and Lave (1972: 60, f. 6) offer the following explanation of stepwise multiple regression:

The predictor variable having the highest zero-order correlation with the dependent variable is entered first, its effect is then partialled out, and the variable having the highest first-order partial correlation with the dependent variable is entered next, and so on.

This process continues until all statistically significant beta weights are determined. The result can be conceived of as an equation with a string of independent variables equal to the dependent variable in the form:

$$Y = a + b_1x_1 + b_2x_2 \ldots + b_nx_n.$$

In this equation Y is the dependent variable, the x's are the various independent variables, the b's are the weights attributed to each explanatory variable, and the a is a constant representing the point at which the regression line crossed the Y axis (Graves and Lave, 1972: 49).

Notes to Chapter 7
The Shaping of Perspective: Consequences of Being Jewish

1. For a correlational analysis, which also introduces control variables for the same data, see Shapiro (1972).

Notes to Appendix

1. Goldstein reported on a study of Toledo, Ohio, in which it was found that 45 to 60 percent of young Jews leave Toledo to live in other cities after they graduate from college (1971: 50). Toledo is a city similar in size to St. Paul both in terms of the total and Jewish populations.

2. The inventory manual reports detailed information on measures of validity (Heist and Yonge, 1968: 28-29) and reliability (1968: 49) for both scales.

Bibliography

Ackerman, Walter I. 1969. Jewish education—for what? *American Jewish Yearbook* 70: 3-36.

Allport, Gordon W. 1954. *The Nature of Prejudice*. Cambridge, Mass.: Wesley.

Ausubel, David P. 1954. *Theory and Problems of Adolescent Development*. New York: Grune and Stratton.

Axelrod, Morris, Floyd J. Fowler and Arnold Gurin. 1967. *A Community Survey for Long Range Planning*. Boston: The Combined Jewish Philanthropics of Greater Boston.

Bem, Daryl J. 1970. *Beliefs, Attitudes and Human Affairs*. Belmont, Calif.: Brooks/Cole.

Ben-Yehuda B. 1966. *La Mahuta Shel Hatodaa Hayehudit*. In Hebrew, tr.: *To the Essence of Jewish Consciousness*. Tel Aviv.

Berger, Peter L. and Thomas Luckmann. 1966. *The Social Construction of Reality*. Garden City, N.Y.: Doubleday.

Biddle, Bruce J. and Edwin J. Thomas. 1966. *Role Theory: Concepts and Research*. New York: Wiley.

Blalock, Hubert M. 1960. *Social Statistics*. New York: McGraw-Hill.

Blau, Peter M. and Otis D. Duncan. 1967. *The American Occupational Structure*. New York: Wiley.

Brenner, Leon O. 1960. "Hostility and Jewish Group Identification." Unpulished Doctoral Treatise, Boston University.

Brodsky, Irving. 1968. Jewish identity and Jewish identification. *Journal of Jewish Communal Service* 44: 254-59.

Calmenson, Jesse B. 1937. Looking back over twenty-five years in St. Paul. *The American Jewish World* Minneapolis-St. Paul, (September 3): T1.

Campbell, Ernest Q. 1969 Adolescent socialization. David A. Goslin (ed.), *Handbook of Socialization Theory and Research*. Chicago: Rand McNally.

Clark, Kenneth B. and Mamie P. Clark. 1958. Racial identification and preference in Negro children. Eleanor E. Maccoby, Theodore M. Newcomb, and Eugene L. Hartley (eds.), *Readings in Social Psychology* (3rd ed). New York: Henry Holt.

Cohen, Herman M., 1952. Rabbi Cohen reviews growth of St. Paul. *The American Jewish World* 41: 7.

Cooley, Charles H. 1909. *Social Organization*. New York: Scribners.

152

Dashefsky, Arnold. 1969. "Social Interaction and Jewish Self-Conception: A Two-Generation Analysis in the St. Paul Community." Unpublished Doctoral Dissertation, University of Minnesota.

_____. 1970. "Interactions and identity: the Jewish Case." Paper presented at the 65th Annual Meeting of the American Sociological Association, New Orleans.

_____. 1971. Being Jewish: an approach to conceptualization and operationalization. Isidore David Passow and Samuel Tobias Lachs (eds.), *Gratz College Anniversary Volume*. Philadelphia: Gratz College.

_____. 1971. A sociological perspective on Jewish identity. Ephraim L. Goldman and Aaron L. Peller (eds.), *Jewish Identity in the 70's*. Philadelphia: The Board of Jewish Education.

_____. 1972. And the search goes on: the meaning of religio-ethnic identity and identification. *Sociological Analysis* 33: 239-45.

_____. and Howard M. Shapiro. 1971. *The Jewish Community of St. Paul*. St. Paul: United Jewish Fund and Council.

de Levita, Daniel J. 1965. *The Concept of Identity*. New York: Basic Books.

Eisenstadt, Shmuel N. 1970. Philip Gillon, Who is a Jew? Quoted p. 7 in *Jerusalem Post* (February 2).

Erikson, Erik H. 1963. *Childhood and Society* (2nd ed.). New York: W. W. Norton.

_____. 1964. *Insight and Responsibility*. New York: W.W. Norton.

Essien-Udom, E.U. 1962. *Black Nationalism; A Search For an Identity in America*. Chicago: University of Chicago Press.

Fainstein, Norman and Stanley Feder. 1966. *Bibliographies on Jewish Identity*. Mimeograph: Massachusetts Institute of Technology.

Festinger, Leon. 1957. A Theory of Cognitive Dissonance. New York: Harper and Row.

Foote, Nelson. 1951. Identification as the basis for a theory of motivation. *American Sociological Review* 16: 14-21.

Freud, Sigmund. 1938. *The Basic Writings of Sigmund Freud*. New York: The Modern Library.

Fuchs, Lawrence H. 1958. Sources of Jewish internationalism and liberalism. Marshall Sklare (ed.), *The Jews*. New York: Free Press.

Gerson, Walter. 1965. Jews at Christmas time. Arnold M. Rose and Caroline B. Rose (eds.), *Minority Problems*. New York: Harper and Row.

Gleason, Philip. 1964. Immigration and American Catholic intellectual life. *The Review of Politics* 26: 147-73.

153

Goldstein, Sidney. 1971. American Jewry, 1970: A demographic profile, *American Jewish Yearbook* 72: 3-88.

————. and Calvin Goldscheider. 1968. *Jewish Americans: Three Generations in a Jewish Community*. Englewood Cliffs, N.J.: Prentice-Hall.

Goffman, Erving. 1963. *Stigma*. Englewood Cliffs, N.J.: Prentice-Hall.

Gordon, Chad. 1968. Self-conception content configurations. Chad Gordon and Kenneth J. Gergen (eds.), *The Self in Social Interaction* New York: Wiley.

Gordon, Louis. 1957. The Center Hebrew School. *The American Jewish World* (September 22): 33.

Gordon, Milton. 1964. *Assimilation in American Life*. New York: Oxford.

Gordon, Milton M. 1969. Marginality and the Jewish intellectual. Peter I. Rose (ed.), *The Ghetto and Beyond*. New York: Random House.

Graves, Theodore D. and Charles A. Lave. 1972. Determinants of urban migrant Indian wages. *Human Organization* 31(1):47-61.

Greenberg, Myron. 1937. Capitol City Hebrew School. *The American Jewish World* (September 3): 33.

Greenberg, Mrs. Philip. 1922. The Capitol City Hebrew School. *The American Jewish World* (September 22): 45.

Hagood, Margaret and Daniel O. Price. 1952. *Statistics for Sociologists* (rev. ed.). New York: Henry Holt.

Hartley, E.L. and M. Rosenbaum and S. Schwartz. 1948. Children's perceptions of ethnic group membership. *Journal of Psychology* 26: 387-98.

Heist, Paul and George Yonge. 1968. *Omnibus Personality Inventory Manual, Form F*. New York: The Psychological Corporation.

Herberg, Will. 1960. *Protestant, Catholic and Jew*. Garden City, N.Y.: Doubleday.

Herman, Simon N. 1970. *American Students in Israel*. Ithaca, N.Y.: Cornell University.

Hess, Sylvan E. 1922. History of the Mt. Zion Hebrew Congregation. *The American Jewish World*, Minneapolis-St. Paul, (September 22): 39.

Hoffman, William. 1957. *Those Were the Days*. Minneapolis: T.S. Dennison.

Hollingshead, August B. 1957. *Two Factor Index of Social Position*. Mimeograph: Yale University.

Ianni, Francis A.J. 1964. Minority group status and adolescent culture. David Gottlieb and C.E. Ramsey, *The American Adolescent*. Homewood, Ill.: Dorsey.

Jewish Liberation Journal. 1969. Editorial (May): 1-2.

154

Kleinman, Philip. 1922. Temple of Aaron Congregation. *The American Jewish World* (September 22): 40.

Kuhn, Manford H. and Thomas S. McPartland. 1954. An empirical investigation of self-attitudes. *American Sociologcial Review* 19: 68-76.

Kuznets, Simon. 1972. *Economic Structure of U.S. Jewry: Recent Trends.* Jerusalem: The Institute of Contemporary Jewry, The Hebrew University.

Laing, R.D. 1967. *The Politics of Experience.* New York: Pantheon Books.

Lazerwitz, Bernard. 1971. Intermarriage and conversion: A guide for future research, *The Jewish Journal of Sociology* 13: 41-63.

Lazerwitz, Bernard. 1970. Contrasting the effects of generation, class, sex, and age on group identification in the Jewish and Protestant communities: *Social Forces* 49: 50-59.

Lewin, Kurt. 1949. *Resolving Social Conflicts.* New York: Harper.

Liebman, Charles S. 1970. Reconstructionism in American Jewish life. *American Jewish Yearbook* 71: 3-99.

Lincoln, Charles Eric. 1961. *The Black Muslims in America.* Boston: Beacon.

Lindesmith, Alfred R. and A.L. Strauss. 1968. *Social Psychology* (3rd ed.). New York: Holt, Rinehart and Winston.

Luckmann, Thomas. 1967. *The Invisible Religion: The Problem of Religion in Modern Society.* New York: Macmillan.

MacKay, Jack B. 1952. Forty years of St. Paul Jewry. *The American Jewish World* (September 28): 11.

_____. 1962. Fifty years of St. Paul Jewry. *The American Jewish World* (September 19): 13.

Makiesky, Jack. 1922. The development of the West Side, St. Paul. *The American Jewish World*, Minneapolis-St. Paul (September 22): 55.

Mannheim, Karl. 1952. *Essays on the Sociology of Knowledge.* London: Routledge.

McCall, George J. and J.L. Simmons. 1966. *Identities and Interaction.* New York: Free Press.

Mead, G.H. 1934. *Mind, Self, and Society.* Chicago: Univeristy of Chicago.

Middleton, Russell and Snell Putney. 1963. Political expression of adolescent rebellion. *American Journal of Sociology* 67: 527-35.

Newman, William M. 1973. *American Pluralism.* New York: Harper and Row.

Nie, Norman H., Dale H. Bent and C. Hadlai Hull. 1970. *Statistical Package for the Social Sciences.* New York: McGraw-Hill.

Offer, D. 1969. *The Psychological World of the Teen-ager*. New York: Basic Books.

Park, Robert Ezra. 1950. *Race and Culture*. Glencoe, Ill.: Free Press.

Parsons, Talcott. 1968. The position of identity in a general theory of action. Chad Gordon and Kenneth J. Gergen (eds.), *The Self in Social Interaction* (1). New York: Wiley.

Parten, Mildred. 1950. *Surveys, Polls, and Samples: Practical Procedures*. New York: Harper.

Phillips, Bernard S. 1966. *Social Research*. New York: MacMillan.

Pinkney, Alphonso. 1969. *Black Americans*. Englewood Cliffs, N.J.: Prentice-Hall.

Plaut, W. Gunther. 1959. *The Jews of Minnesota*. New York: American Jewish Historical Society.

Report of the National Advisory Commission on Civil Disorders. 1968. New York: Bantam.

Rose, Arnold M. and Caroline, B. Rose (eds.). 1965. *Minority Problems*. New York: Harper and Row.

Rose, Arnold M. 1967. *Sociology* (2nd ed., revised). New York: Alfred A. Knopf.

Rosen, Bernard C. 1965. *Adolescence and Religion*. Cambridge, Mass.: Schenkman.

Roshwald, Mordecai. 1970. "Who is a Jew in Israel?" *The Jewish Journal of Sociology* 12: 233-66.

Roth, Phillip. 1967. *Portnoy's Complaint*. New York: Random House.

Rutchik, Allen. 1968. Self-Esteem and Jewish identification. *Jewish Education* 38: 40-46.

Sachar, Howard M. 1958. *The Course of Modern Jewish History*. New York: Dell.

Sartre, Jean-Paul. 1948. *Anti-Semite and Jew*. New York: Schocken 1948.

Sebald, Hans. 1968. *Adolescence: A Sociological Analysis*. New York: Appleton-Century-Crofts.

Segalman, Ralph. 1966. "Self-Hatred Among Jews: A Test of the Lewinian Hypothesis of Marginality of Jewish Leadership." Umpublished Doctoral Dissertation, New York University.

_____. 1967. Jewish identity scales: a report. *Jewish Social Studies* 29: 92-111.

Shapiro, Howard M. 1969. "Marginality, Familial Interaction, and Intellectuality: The Shaping of Perspective in a Jewish Community." Unpublished Doctoral Dissertation, University of Minnesota.

_____. 1972. Jewish identification and intellectuality: a two generation analysis. *Sociological Analysis* 33: 230-38.

_____. and Arnold Dashefsky. 1974. Religious education and ethnic identification in a Jewish community. *Review of Religious Research* 15: 93-102.

_____ and Robert Gliner. 1972. *Human Perspectives*. New York: Free Press.

Shapiro, Judah J. 1970. New aspects of American Jewry. *Jewish Frontier* 37 (7): 11-16.

Sherman, Charles B. 1961. *The Jew Within American Society: A Study in Ethnic Individuality*. Detroit: Wayne State University.

Shibutani, Tamotsu. 1955. Reference groups as perspectives. *American Journal of Sociology* 60: 562-69.

Sieber, Sam D. 1973. The integration of fieldwork and survey methods. *American Journal of Sociology* 78: 1335-59.

Simpson, George E. and J. Milton Yinger. 1972. *Racial and Cultural Minorities: An Analysis of Prejudice and Discrimination*. New York: Harper and Row.

Sklare, Marshall. 1972. *Conservative Judaism: An American Religious Movement*. New York: Schocken.

_____. 1971. *America's Jews*. New York: Random House.

_____. 1969. The ethnic church and the desire for survival. Peter I. Rose (ed.), *The Ghetto and Beyond*. New York: Random House.

_____. and Joseph Greenblum. 1967. *Jewish Identity on the Suburban New Frontier*. New York: Basic Books.

Stern, Kenneth. 1969. Is religion necessary? Peter I. Rose (ed.), *The Ghetto and Beyond*. New York: Random House.

Stone, Gregory P. 1962. Appearance and the self. Arnold M. Rose (ed.), *Human Behavior and Social Processes*. Boston: Houghton Mifflin.

Stryker, Sheldon. 1964. The interactional and situational approaches. Harold T. Christensen (ed.), *Handbook of Marriage and the Family*. Chicago: Rand McNally.

Uris, Leon. 1958. *Exodus*. Garden City, N.Y.: Doubleday.

Van Den Haag, Ernest. 1969. *The Jewish Mystique*. New York: Stein and Day.

Wigoder, Geoffrey. 1968. How Jewish are Americans? *Jerusalem Post* (May 10): 11.

Winch, Robert F. 1962. *Identification and Its Familial Determinants*. Indianapolis: Bobbs-Merrill.

Wirth, Louis. 1928. *The Ghetto*. Chicago, Ill.: University of Chicago.

Yarrow, Marion R. 1958. Personality development and minority group membership. Marshall Sklare (ed.) *The Jews*. Glencoe, Ill.: Free Press.

Index

Index

Absolutism, sense of, 6-7
Acculturation, patterns of, 17, 86, 101
Ackerman, Walter I., cited, 57
Adath Israel orthodox congregation, 27
Adolescense: activities of, 64, 70, 73;
 experiences in, 78-81; fathers', 81-84;
 and formative years, 67; period of,
 52-58, 117-118, 124, 140; and
 socialization, 2-3, 78; stress of, 131; in
 Yorktown, 36
Adults: attitudes and values, 53; 67;
 consciousness of, 43; education
 courses for, 21; experiences and
 activities, 52, 61; young, 107-108, 131
Africa, class system in, 1
Age, factor of, 4, 49, 77-78
Agudas Achim Synagogue, 19
Aid, overseas, 20
Alien societies, 100, 129
Ambiguity, tolerance of, 108-109, 114
American Jewish Archives, 148
American Jewish World, 148
American Jewish Yearbook, 18
Amish, the, 1
Amos, prophet, 129
Anglo-Jewish weekly press, 134, 148
Antidefamation League of B'nai B'rith,
 19-20, 30
Anti-Semitism: effects of, 19-20, 108; overt,
 44; rise of, 20; specter of, 30, 127-128;
Apartheid system, 1
Aphorisms, rabbinical, 121
Arab-Israeli War, 43. *See also* Six Day War
 of 1967
Arab states, 41; terrorists of, 127
Archives, Jewish, 148
Art exhibits, 30
Assimilation, ethnic, 85-86, 101, 103
Atheism, 122
Austrian-Jews, 40
Ausubel, David P., cited, 33, 131
Authority, societal, 129
Axelrod, Morris, cited, 46

Banks and banking, profession of, 19
Bar Mitzvah, celebration of, 40
Behavior and characteristics, appropriate,
 4-5, 51, 56-57, 68
Beliefs and attitudes, 3, 38, 43-44, 48-53,
 56-57, 67-68, 81, 95, 112, 138-140
Bem, Daryl J., cited, 54
Ben-Yehuda, B., cited, 8
Berger, Peter L., cited, 93
Beth Israel orthodox congregation, 27

Bible, reading of, 14, 28
Biddle, Bruce J., cited, 53
Black Muslim organization, 51
Black Panther movement, 51
Blacks: community organizations, 1, 51, 129;
 in St. Paul, 23; student groups, 51
Blalock, Hubert M., cited, 61
Blau, Peter M., cited, 34
B'nai B'rith Lodge, 19-20, 30
B'nai Zion Synagogue, 16
Boston, Mass., 46
Brenner, Leon O., cited, 8
B'rith Abraham Synagogue, 16
Brodsky, Irving, cited, 8, 61
Brother Daniel, case of, 7
Brothers, influence of, 82-83, 119, 140; older,
 54-55, 62, 73, 75, 91-92
Bund, The, 16
Bureaucracy and bureaucrats, 39, 77, 115
Businesses, family owned, 19, 77, 126

Calmenson, Jesse B., cited, 17, 20
Campbell, Ernest Q., cited, 53
Capitol Hill, district of, 17, 20; Hebrew
 School, 16,18
Careers, planning of, 29. *See also*
 Occupations
Cemeteries, Jewish, 12-13
Census, Bureau of, 18
Center Hebrew School, 18, 20
Central Communal afternoon school, 28
Central High School, 23-26
Charity, 94, funds for, 13, 26
Chauvinism, 6
Chevre Mishna Ashkanas synagogue, 19
Chicago, Jews in, 37, 72, 76, 81
Chicanos minority groups, 51
Child-centeredness, 117; parent interaction,
 117-118, 129, 131;
Childhood, background and early years, 52,
 76, 81, 108, 117-118, 129
Children of God religious organization, 51
Christian religion, 7, 17, 128. *See also* Gentile
 relationships
Christmas, observance of, 42, 48, 138-141
Chutzpah, 115
Citizenship, acquiring of, 7
Civic organizations, membership in, 19
Clark, Kenneth B., cited, 52
Clerical occupations, 25
Cohen, Herman M., cited 17, 20, 40
College, attendance at, 33, 36, 41, 49, 68, 77,
 145. *See also* Education
Coolidge, Calvin, 95

About the Authors

Arnold Dashefsky is Professor of Sociology and Director of the Center for Judaic Studies and Contemporary Jewish Life at the University of Connecticut. He studied at the Hebrew University and Hayim Greenberg College in Jerusalem and at Gratz College in Philadelphia, where he earned the Bachelor of Hebrew literature. He received the B.A. and the M.A. from Temple University and the Ph.D. from the University of Minnesota. Professor Dashefsky has taught at Temple University, Pennsylvania State University at Ogontz, and the University of Minnesota. He is currently president of the Association for the Social Scientific Study of Jewry.

Howard M. Shapiro is Director of Dover Mental Health Associates and specializes in helping individuals, families, and organizations from a social psychological perspective. He received the B.A. from Brandeis University, the M.A. from Boston University, and the Ph.D. from the University of Minnesota. Dr. Shapiro has previously taught at the University of Minnesota, George Washington University, and the University of New Hampshire. Currently he conducts workshops and seminars for both public and private organizations.